Georgia Brown's Great Escape

Poetry by

D. J. Andersen

Art attribution

Cover art by D. J. Andersen

Photography by Jean Reid

Dedication

To the memory of

Georgia Ann Brown.

Georgia Brown, December 1953

The woman who showed me that courage was necessary and that escape is possible. D. J. A.

Contents

5

MAY

it was May for eighty days.

malingering.

some sun.

some not.

songbirds sang and rivers flowed soft silk.

in June,

which wasn't yet.

I welcomed occasional rain.

others sat on their front porch swings

all the May song days.

I loved the sad September.

watching weaving women trees

make multi-colored quilts of leaves

for dying grasses. the

beginning of a dirge and burial for May.

GRANDMOTHERS

hawk-nosed grandma sneaks downstairs at night when
she thinks no one is looking. getting down on wrinkled hands and knobby,
bony knees, she is looking for the dreams she dropped earlier in the day,
she hasn't found them. she wears a scattered urgency at her loss.
we told her not to feed the terrier chicken bones, she doesn't listen.
her own mother once prepared the dining room table for the soldiers
who never came, but never mind. she made lemonade, so sour, so
they would not be thirsty anymore. pitchers in a row stood up on
her best white tablecloth with the empty glasses and napkins piled.
tired of waiting for them, she'd run out the door in the front of the
brick house. come back later with an apron full of hard candies she had
stolen. we all knew she did it, but she cursed at us in interwoven
English-German, and we were silenced.   grandma whose dreams were lost
stuck
her one pointing finger out and shook it, scolding. later, she poured all the
pitchers of too
sour lemonade down the kitchen sink drain.
it unclogged the plumbing and led to leaking one day.

drip.

drop.

with the terrier dead, the plumber said the leaking was due to the pouring
of sweet or sour lemonade down the drain, he said someone had to
stop it. he would only fix it free for one time. with his knees pressed down
on top dried chicken bones, great grandma stared him down while
while she sucked toothlessly on a yellow lemon drop.

FISH

picnic in the sunny green grass yard at grandma's house.
Mommy was helping other grown-ups place bowls of food and
plates of hotdogs and hamburgers on all the picnic tables.

I walked along the stony bank by the silver creek
while they busied themselves, my bare feet toes
covered with wet-dry clumps, saw a long-thin fish I
almost stepped on. Poor fish, it must be hungry.

fish only drank water, I reasoned, and behind my
Mommy's back I snatched a long green bean from the bean salad bowl,
ran back to feed the fish some food.

"here, fish, I brought you a bean",
gently slid it down the fish's mouth into its' throat,
waited……..

"eat. Please, eat, mr. fish". I begged it. fish was making me sad.

Grandpa came then, to see what trouble I was getting into
down by the creek alone.

"what are you doing? That fish is dead. Go wash your hands!"
He picked the poor fish up by its' tail and threw it into the silvery water,
the green bean hanging out of its' mouth with no teeth.

Teeth! No teeth! That's why it couldn't eat the bean!
I gave it the wrong food.

Grandpa had murdered the fish when he threw it away, and I tried to
ask mommy what dead was, but she was eating food

and chewing it up with her teeth.

11

FIRST TAKE

the morning air has washed itself, preparing

for coming grace with an orange orb rising.

all seen is wet and squeaky clean from

this to that horizon.

as branches, leaves shake themselves

of dew dropped in the night,

the sun bursts out, ecstatic,

from the binding rind of night.

BIRDS

black tees square the sky

in circular flight.

formation:

fly right, then

dive into the sunset.

flush against a breathless blue,

ballet below the sky.

the trees nod, awed

at first, then rise to

a standing ovation.

FIRE

there were no smoke signals for days,

I grew nervous, waiting. any time

someone could sneak up behind me, slice my throat with a knife.

slice it open.

my name was Running Wolf,

but I could not name my father.

no.

I cannot name my father.

the blustery winds blew hard from the north.

the blizzardy sheets of snow stung my chapped face.

I gathered bark strips for a fire,

cut firewood, broke branches off hapless trees.

I knew I had to keep my fire lit, blowing sparks,

fire fairies up high into the night.

to keep the fire alive, the fire lit

by my ancestors, the fire that lit my veins,

the fire that would send me a smoke signal

soon.

NEW YEAR'S MORNING

I closed the door quickly

jesus it was cold out there.

slight snow falling up onto the grey porch steps.

why

when I was out there

did I not notice it before?

I shoveled snow out of the driveway

wearing only socks to cover my feet.

it did not seem to be unusual.

my beloved dog cowers at the harsh word "NO!." but I did not

know what else to say to make her stop it.

the heat in this small place I fill is not much.

not nearly enough to keep me warm as

I wait and wait for you to call.

I am aware now, of my shaking.

I shiver.

playing computer games I do not win.

my cigarette smoke floats. a snaky cloud in the air of this room,

I watch it float

to the birdcage, to the outer room and

off beyond.

the words of a Springsteen song, not freezing solid,

strings that stretch into sentences all across my inside head.

maybe six hours till the snowstorm of white ice flakes

catching the light just right.

coming with a roar, as always, to scare all to stay put in their houses.

right now.

the weather is all right.

MURDER

stopped quick.

on the landing of the stairs.

heart pounding, I put my hand over it so it would not make noise.

someone down there in the basement.

I heard noise.

crept softly down, keeping my feet on the sides of the stairs

and not the middles.

middles creak.

at the bottom of the stairs I looked for the intruder who

made noise.

there.

sitting in a black rocking chair,

watching television,

Eileen sat.

her hair done up like Norman's mother's.

this was not our house.

neither she nor me should be there.

confused, I watched and thought.

she did not see nor hear me.

surprise that

sudden unstoppable rage ran all the way up my spine,

with no warning.

hammer. on the pegboard

on the wall.

right-handed swing hit her just above the ear.

she

turned, then.

sprung up.

from her rocking rocker, hands reaching out to

choke me.

not.

this.

time.

I hammer whacked the other side of her head so hard she

fell.

down.

on the cement floor hard.

I jumped down.

most people jump up.

sitting on top her chest, I beat her.

beat her.

beat her.

rivers of blood ran with glee all over the floor,

her blood spit sprayed my face and hair. I

loved the warm feel of it, even though

I had to wipe my eyes clear with my bloody shirt sleeve so

I could see her. I

could not stop, I

beat her face to a mashed pulp, I

was red with redemption and glory, so

close to heaven I cried.

finally.

after the fury.

I laid my hammer down.

stood up dripping.

woke up dry.

CHRISTMAS EVE

on Christmas Eve,

I'm going to sit

on my couch, find a

t.v. station, listen

to Christmas carols.

watch the singers of songs and

silently pray.

not out loud.

for salvation

that may never come.

feel in my heart to find

the meaning I have lost

that used to calm me,

pray to be washed clean

of sins I am not sure are mine.

BILLIE

When Gayle's dad sold the house away from Billie, I saw her on the street
begging for shelter. But the only thing they did and said it was for her own
good was to cut down all the giant trees which had always lined that street
side, behind
the street curb.

Gayle's dad was explaining about the trap door to the basement. He was the
yellow-toothed betrayer, his eyes green now at the thought of all the
money he would
finally have.

I stepped over Billie's body in the laundromat, I was making change by the
Tide machine so I could catch the North Kent bus to go home with my
freshly clean
clothing.

And sure, I felt bad about it all, christ, she needed to be buried , but I
had never liked her much and there was nothing I could do.

Later, later that week I went back to Gayle's dad's attic to get my boxes and
boxes of books and dishes I had packed up years before to just store, and I
didn't see the reason for it anymore, the attic was filthy and the boxes
crusted with dirt, and one rainy summer night Gayle flew right into a red
rage as she was driving over to drop off
Benny the Rat. Keep your goddamn stuff, she hissed.

Billie could have holed up in the attic on those freezing winter nights, I guess
nobody ever thought about it. The fiberglass insulation had never been
properly installed or finished in the attic, it hung from the rafters and was
peeling off all the walls as if it too, knew
it was not needed now.

BUBBLE BATH

it was the same day Charles came home from the vet

who'd cut off my dog's tail.

horrified, I chased him through the rooms, a people

bandaid in my hand so I could cover it up.

Charles growled at me and grandpa said it didn't hurt.

if I chased him, he would bite me.

that evening, grandma ran bath water in the claw foot tub,

said we didn't have any bubble bath, left me alone in the bathroom

with its' green press and stick, one bent towel rack.

I'd make bubbles, then.

plenty of stuff underneath the bathroom sink cabinet.

cleanser, blue stuff for the toilet bowl, a little bit of

bleach, grandma's white shampoo. I

emptied it all. everything into the bath water and

saw bubbles.

grabbed my washrag folded, stepped into the water, sat down.

screamed.

my mommy came to the hospital as the white clad

big nosed man looked at my out loud burns.

mommy held my hand, asked what had I been thinking.

bubbles, mom.

THE PAINTING

my third grade teacher, she made fun of me all

the time.

and Susan, too.

she'd put coins in her mouth.

teacher created an art contest.

we could use pencils or brushes to draw or paint.

I painted.

the biggest apple tree

I could fit on the paper.

biggest reddest apples in the world. the tree

was brown with many branches, the

sky was black.

teacher held my painting I was proud of up to the whole class,

said

no.

no.

no.

blue is the color of the skies over apple trees, maybe

with a white fluffy cloud.

I stood up.

defiant.

hands clenched.

told her

out loud.

no.

my skies are black.

ROBIN

it was me and merry and connie, slouching out on the lower porch steps.
kenny ordered pizza, we were grabbin' and grinnin'at such a treat, our
fingers and faces greasy as we gobbled.

someone said where is robin, and I certainly didn't know or even care.
merry was plottin' with kenny on how she could get out tonight to go with
kenny somewhere, I
wasn't really listening to details because I didn't care about that either.

there was robin, walking down the driveway, there wasn't any pizza left for
her.

we saw the blood, all the red running down her shirt, her shorts, dripping
from her
hands, it made spots on the gravel, we stopped, stared, sat still. her tear
stained

eyes picked out me. And I thought no, please don't, not me, I can't, as she
held her
slashed wrists out to me I didn't want to see, just not to see, why?

why me?
me and merry had stuffed a sock in her mouth once and tied her up,
dragged her
ass out to the back yard to lie there in the sun, not able to even call for

Help.

thieving bitch had gone into our room and stole my eyebrow tweezers. Me
and merry
climbed the tree up to the garage roof, drank bottled cokes as we laughed
and sunned.

it was that I couldn't stand her staring a hole in me, I put my sock-stuffing arm around her
and calmly led her inside to the bathroom sink. Cold water over the wrists wounds to stop
the bleeding, then bandaged her

feeling a reverential calm that came from nowhere and somewhere as I walked her over
to the open gate across the parking lot to the children's home clinic, where they kept
her safe from herself at least for overnight, but not safe from

Herself.

when I got home, the house mother awaited, scolding me for not telling her about
robin first. The other girls in a group inside wanting to know what happened and
what did she say to me.

I said robin slit her wrists that's all I know, my calm all gone, my mind askew.

PROMISES BROKEN

she said please don't.

I am so afraid. I

criss-crossed my heart and

promised not to.

I was wrong to promise.

the pain that sears at promises broken hurts beyond comprehension.

I knew that all along.

she sobbed so hard for such a long time

I felt the very maw of madness near me.

sobs that fell one on top the other, rolled off the bed in a heap.

she fell down into a stark dark madness, not

slowly, or by degrees, but.

all at once quickly.

she saw things involving people she knew, but those things never happened.

she heard voices talk to her from the t.v., they told her to do things crazy,

like getting an extra room key for a room that was not her own. she said

she knew the people who'd checked in there at the motel, and wanted to

visit.

she cursed me in a mad voice,

her face pressed up against the glass window of my past, pressed

so hard, she flattened her nose.

teardrops fell from her loony eyes.

I needed to be cursed.

the one

who broke promises

to a once tender, still fragile

heart.

so

I welcomed the curses.

I stood up and took them all,

blood dripping from my promise-breaking hands.

Jerry said she should be committed somewhere, I

said no.

Sandy asked me never to bring her with me again,

I had to promise.

in New Orleans, later, when she was practically dead,

I tried.

to belatedly

sincerely, truly,

fervently, sadly

full of regret, shamed.

apologize.

she put her hand over my mouth to stop

my words from getting out to keep my mouth from forming an

apology for promises broken.

she could not get enough air into her lungs to cry or even reply.

so I laid it gently in her lap as she sat sleeping on the sad train home.

THE LADDER

because I walked all the way down to

the forbidden creek, where I didn't think anyone could see me,

Grandma burst out the back door, screaming

about germs and wet and drowning and dirty and said

she was gonna switch me.

I watched her crack off a long slender tree branch, while she

was peeling off it's leaves, I

ran across the yard and up the ladder left leaning against the garage,

holding on real tight rung by rung till I got to the top all the way to the roof.

Safe.

And so high, I could see the world.

Grandma stood so far down there, said please come down, and

she looked scared but I didn't know why—she had

the whipping switch in her right hand, it was waiting for me.

Grandma said I would fall off and crack my head, but

I thought that would be silly. I had no intention of falling off the ladder.

Grandma ran into the house, and after a long time when I

had already peed my toddler pants, my grandpa came. He climbed up the ladder,

Wrapped his warm flannel-shirted arms around me.

Safe.

THE STORM

I have always been chained to my being ,
Being one long screaming essence flying through space
fast like light years or the speed of sound or motion undetectable
To the naked eye. A smile forced into my face from the

Terrible wind of falling flying falling flying--like the picture of
Jules and me screaming down the Mean Streak roller coaster at Cedar Point.

at only six, I clung to the lone waif tree in the front dark yard because of the
ferocious storm
In my nightmare--which was already black and wet and the rain was
drowning me while the
winds long strong hands tried to pry my fingers from my grip.

At ten, I drank straight down, bottoms up, my first double shot of vodka.
The wonderful warming inside as it ran down into the rivers of me.

The rivers of me, surviving the storm.

THE SOARING MACHINE

foster parents bought me a red tricycle from Sears,

said I could only ride it on the sidewalk plapped down

in front of the house.

that

was not much fun.

when I made sure they were not looking,

I pushed the trike up to the very top of the hilly driveway.

sit.

get ready.

GO!

I sailed!

I soared!

I laughed out loud!

I nearly left the ground and flew like a bird before

crashing into the street curb on the other side.

foster parents put my tricycle away in the basement for two weeks.

they said I could never do that.

I could have been killed.

hit by a car.

hurt in my crash.

I forlornly played.

had a doll.

jumped rope.

it was not the same.

at night in my bed, with the covers pulled up to my chin,

in the silent and dark house I could only

think about the next time.

so excited.

me and my red soaring machine.

FALLING DOWN

mom so tall.

her midnight hair falling down around her shoulders.

looking up at her,

I felt small.

it was the darkest road to nowhere I had ever seen.

black asphalt and not one car drove by us.

mom held my small hand so tight.

I had to pee so bad, but

mommy said to hold it ten minutes.

that was as long as three or four days,

but I tried 'cause mom had been crying.

she lifted me up in her arms after the fight, walked with me out the front door.

I felt the warm pee run down my legs inside my pants,

mom didn't scold me because she looked so sad.

I would have held her, but we were walking too fast on and on

down the dark road to Aunt Flossie's, she said.

my peed legs got cold. me and mom walking to

find me dry pants at Flossie's,

but I didn't see her house anywhere.

it was the dark long road, the walk of my lifetime.

MUST BE LIKE HEAVEN

I looked out from under the glare of the hot sun, so stooped and weeding,

thirsty and not allowed in the house for water.

just in time to see Kevin's mother bend down and hug him.

I desperately wanted her to hug me, too

since she knew how to do it.

please please please please.

hug me.

knowing, realistically.

that it would never happen.

I imagined, then.

two arms wrapped around my body,

holding me close and tender.

it must be like heaven.

heaven.

SNATCHED

sunny day summer,

certain.

maybe July.

me playing in the green grass backyard lawn,

with toys I can't remember.

grandma hanging clean clothes from a blue basket on

the overhead clothesline, pinching them with clothespins.

then.

the social worker I remembered from sometime before came.

she drove her rusty ford up the driveway, making

crickly cracklies sounds with her tires over gravel.

she blew out of her green rusty car door yelling at grandma for not

having made me ready at eleven o'clock. grandma yelled back, but

she had to, had to

pack up all my clothes and toys in boxes, she had to hurry, and

I stood in the living room, attached to Mrs. Pickerel's hand, or else

I would have runned and hid away hard.

social worker stuffed me in the car with my boxes

going to mommy's, I asked, hopeful.

no.

but I want mommy.

no.

going to stay with really nice new people.

don't want nice people.

especially new ones.

want my mommy.

I couldn't cry, couldn't sob, couldn't talk.

too many great big grief lumps choking me in my throat.

grandma standing in front of the back porch, arms so

fiercely folded across her chest, not waving back at me as

the house disappeared behind the trees lining the road.

tall pines and some silver maples.

I slid all the way down in my seat in the back of the car,

to see if I could be invisible.

DONELL

I think

I thought she loved me.

she sat so small on the edge of her bed one day, held

her hands over ears to shut out the shut out the screams I

formed as Eileen beat me in the same room, she

Donell , screamed too, she cried out, "I

CAN'T TAKE IT ANY MORE!" tears in torrents puddling in her lap.

Eileen ignored her, but

I think

I thought that Eileen loved her.

black and white sketches, vivid life-sized paintings of reds

and purples and oranges are in my mind where they stay.

they are the memories of Donell in turmoil.

the horror she saw, the terror she hid,

the molestation she

could not stop.

the so secret sobbing

she was alone. all

alone.

and I

behind my high walls where I

lived in my fortress.

knights held bows and arrows at the gates, I.

could not reach my arms out far enough to

comfort her. Inside my world of daydreams, most

times I did not see her at all. I

see her in the photographs I have.

I rode a mechanical horse, it jumped so high over the cyclone fence

Eileen imprisoned us in and ran so fast I was in the west by sundown,

oiling the horse joints, building a campfire, laying out my sleeping bag.

but.

I told,

I told everyone at the Children's Home, and I

shouted out to the whole wide weary world to please take

Donell out. out and away from that place that was not a home, and

when I told of the molestation, especially,

THEY DID! THEY ORDERED IT BE DONE.

OR ELSE!

she lived with her dad in a small house on Rose Avenue,

it burned down after they moved out.

Donell married and went away but

I think

I thought she loved me.

we were bonded, scarred, burned through together.

weren't we? I'd helped save her, didn't I?

She never forgave me for that.

after years and years and miles and miles of stepping so blindly

in and out of her life, watching the dullness in her eyes,

one. of the days. she unzipped her carelessness and showed me.

she did not make a place for me anywhere inside her life.

from her, I was alone. all

alone.

I am so very wrong when

I think

I thought she loved me.

she did not.

THE OTHERS

I did not.

do anything

to

deserve the

battering, beating, bashing, burning, torture, molestation, cutting, slapping, starving ,

hurting, hate, rape, dry-firing, madness, meanness, isolation, slavery, submission, harm.

after adoption,

they had one great chance to make me their child.

maybe, but not likely, to take the places

vacated by my mother and father.

they tossed the great chance out the kitchen window,

into the back yard where it mingled with the growing grasses and random rabbit shit.

I

have often

wondered,

wanting

to know

where evil

begins.

was it a Monday night, say, while washing dinner dishes, that she was entered

by a wandering demonic entity? was she aware of it, did she give it
permission?

was it a choice, chance, a

malignancy like cancer?

some of us get it, others don't.

did the malevolent ever cause her pause,

halt, hesitation?

she was a bigamist once.

did bigamy lead to evil, or did evil lead to bigamy?

I study the pictures.

some in faded color, some in grainy black and white,

of me wearing a reddish dress, stick thin legs in

my beloved cowboy boots,

staring down at the floor, like I was looking for a bug,

the others.

sad Buck in suspenders, unseen Sue, taller Nancy, once fatter Freda,

the ever

preserved Donell.

they were all of them

removed from

that house.

those lucky children, but not me.

after all the years of still not knowing

I am only sure of one thing.

Jack was evil before he was born.

he lies face down on the heated floor of hell.

all but one of all the others whom

evil entered and possessed are piled on top of him,

giving him no room to move

and no chance of ever getting out

of hell.

THE TORTOISE

jack brought the tortoise as big as the state

of Rhode Island. he said he found it

in the road, so proud of himself for

a reason I did not understand.

eileen put it inside a metal bucket on the slab stone patio

poured water over it, fed it lettuce left over from our supper salad.

I saw the tortoise. I wondered how to comfort it.

should I pet it's shell or caress it's head?

I didn't know, so

I did nothing.

I think it was sad, it's legs against the bucket sides,

no room to walk or move, head stuck up to escape

the water, remembering tortoise things.

when winter came, the tortoise froze to death

no one came to save the captured animal.

I think they just forgot about it, forgetting

being more convenient.

I imagined me being the tortoise thrown

in a cold metal bucket, the frost coming.

being alive, scratching at the bucket prison

with its tortoise claws. feeling the cold that crept

into it's eyes, wanting to go home. then freezing

slowly

or quickly

to death.

I kicked the bucket once

with the toe of my winter boot.

furious at the death it held.

OUT THERE

I have panic disorder and cannot read out loud.

I have believed that it was my fault.
other people have believed it, too—they have kindly or impatiently
tried to give me lessons on how to read out loud.

but I cannot speak well, and sometimes, often,
not at all as my throat closes up, my heart gallops away
a horse racing on a track like the ones my father works at.

sometimes drunk makes it go away for a little while.
my father says I am not living up to my potential,
my mother told my brother I am sometimes strange, and so

she sees it. they all see it.

Gayle left me stranded in McDonald's parking lot, rolled
down her window, said I just better get over it
when the panic came from nowhere, no reason
nothing to fear, I had to get out of the building
after our order was placed.

I cannot run without falling down.

the counselor called it "anxiety" and gave me valium
I overdosed on purpose
because it's not, it's not, it's panic

I have shopped in grocery stores, that's
where I go to buy my food, the heads of lettuce stiffen me
so I must leave my grocery cart, and walk as best as
fast as I can walk without breathing out there,

Out.
Out.
Out.

It's people.
It's places.
It's panic.
It's purple.

It pins me.

DRIFTWOOD

love, I floundered.

a scaly fish on the beach

when I should have been in the lake.

be friends, talk on the cordless phone about

our cats and their comedy.

I walked as noiselessly as I could, down the dark roads,

wearing my shiny black jump boots all the way.

when night arrives unannounced in the middle of the day,

the sun cannot be yellow.

maybe I had dues to pay.

If I had debt out

standing, I was truly not living, just

going on and on endlessly out of daily habit in the same way

I walked on and on along the beach, looking for only

the water polished stones, ignoring the tides and the driftwood.

MID-WINTER LOSS

it is, perhaps,

my greatest loss.

that I did not, when I had the chance.

the time.

to hold you dearly close and hard, to

soothe you, protect you, love you, tell you.

a vacancy that cannot be filled

lies broken in the far past, but

I carry it with me now, it surfaces once more and against my will.

I did not know how to.

it is on and on mid-winter winds blowing out my failure

so I can see it.

time does not necessarily pass because I did not cherish you, my darling.

it becomes a crash, a pile-up on RT 63, or Deerfield Circle,

an over and over again layering that is not stopped by remembrance.

so high. even on a ladder I cannot see over the top,

to where there is wonder.

a clear, uncluttered, precious, once-in-a-life time air.

a sadness lies in the corner of our once great house.

it is not to be moved.

THE TELLING

to talk.

about it.

began to break me down, so

I spoke in short and quiet half and halting sentences so

I wouldn't, maybe, fall out of myself and drown like

a terrible wall of ice rejected by the iceberg and falling oh so far down

Down.

Into the water.

splash so big it hands itself to heaven.

to tell about the evil ones,

to tell them how he made me suck it took me

over a once-cleared path now suckled and lush, trees moved out

to block my way, I

Stood.

remembering behind my eyes.

Immobilized.

What was I doing wrong?

 wrong wrong wrong.

I screamed inside

Out to the oceans into the depth cried into rivers held up arms held pled to

God.

so.

I started

to stop

the telling.

HAPPINESS

when my lovers asked me are you happy have I

made you happy I. could not reply, I got stuck.

gears in head stopped. so I hurried on to say

yes, yes, yes. I am so happy. you complete me.

knowing that behind the words I spoke

there lived a liar. happiness never happened

to me.

at all.

I did not know what it was I

needed to feel.

was it short, round, red, long, deep, wet, thin, bubbly, religious, invisible?

where did happiness stay?

did it live in the heart, mind, mouth?

could it be held, maybe lovingly caressed?

did it come to everyone but me?

what about thieves and robbers and molesters,

murderers, drug addicts, alcoholics, homeless, slaves?

were they ever happy?

did happiness live in the dark or the light, in the cold or the warm?

could happiness be eaten, worn, wrinkled, or blue?

for a long green tense time the lovers came and went away to

find happiness in others, after seeing it not in me.

one day.

I held a happiness,

I beheld it,

I recognized it,

I knew the all the answers to all my questions,

weeping with long lost joy

I dearly

held it so hard against my beating heart that

I broke it.

since then,

I sit in a green lawn chair on the brick patio outside,

I watch the river run on and on, knowing

I don't want any more of happiness.

MARCH 2nd

she said that you were brave.

you were a tiger.

you said you were not afraid of love.

you lied to me, you.

failed her, too.

not thinking, not caring about what your lie would cost me.

my god my life my aching. shredded tears. deafness.

muteness, shock. needing salve for by heart bled into all the

oceans, fishes swimming away from that torrent. later.

all codes entering my brain would stop. I live in

an ice house now and have ice eyes. I cannot form my

mouth into expression with my ice lips. I no longer

move, I do not grow. I never go outside into the sun.

blood that once ran all around my body in veins changed

into something solid. I wonder, momentarily, if my heart

still beats inside me. sometimes.

MARCH 4th

she said, her

friend said that Dixie was a miracle.

wasn't she?

not

my miracle.

miracle rattled around in my head

like small stones in a tin can.

I will never forgive me

for my spastic moment.

because she cut me

into so many pieces, leaving me the rest of my life only

because she could not take that too, to find and collect them

all. nothing to hold them together with.

and I could lose some of them forever,

becoming only parts of who I'd been

before her.

I sob,

I cannot find the sun.

frantic, the marrow of my bones

is leaking out.

she shreds heartbeat.

I put my ear to my chest so I can hear the damage done.

I cannot make it through this. I cannot

make it through this. I will be with you,

she said. with you with me. I

cannot make it through this. all

the sounds of life are getting fainter.

my friends are silent.

they do not want to add to or subtract me.

I find no comfort there.

I keep holding my breath because I do not know what to do with it.

she said one time.

I taught her how to fly.

I was not aware of it.

she will tell all the others how hard she tried to help me.

help me.

she did.

help me.

break down.

MARCH 8TH

walked way over to the torn blue curtain, pulled it back

long enough to see spring huddled briefly, like a cold

stray canine. so. I sat back down in the dining room chair,

where I folded a Lipton tea tag into a small wetted ball.

You should not sit as you sit in that great wood

captain's chair. you sit with threat in your hands, you

grow to enormous out of proportions, you open

your mouth and the room turns to ice.

I will not come to the ice room after drawing class today,

that whitest place you call an office.

it's infested with words you don't control, words

who bite and sting.

it's polluted with the callous air you wear around you for

your own protection. You fill it up with your own monsters,

and you know it isn't fair.

I came to you.

MARCH 14th

you said my posture was defiant and

I wondered, how is that possible?

it was my round-shouldered slouch I wore while walking

to you, to make myself smaller than Alice.

you told me never say the cat has got your tongue and

I thought how is that possible?

you said I failed, not being all that you expected.

once expected. and I wondered if it was my fault

that you had expectations of me.

one time at Wendy's, I remembered you said you could not

think. of how to go on without me, yet.

you did go on and on so effortlessly.

I rose up and stood, staring at your fish, your plant, your framed

workshop certificates. that must be how you define yourself to all

of those who enter and look at them, too.

I turned my back on you and opened the exit door, you said.

you deserved a better response that that.

fine.

go find one.

MARCH 17th

if you'd never worn that silly Wyatt Earp suit on Valentine's Day,

standing by the window

allowing the sun to make shadows out of your face,

I never would have entertained thoughts of suicide by bicycle.

if I hadn't accepted the strawberries picked by your mother's hand

from her own garden then packed up in a picnic basket,

I could not have worked the Centipedes machine so hard so long in the
arcade.

if you hadn't walked me in the wind our one November day.

I would not have jammed my fists so far down in my jeans pocket.

standing alone in the dark hallway after the windstorms blew out

everything in range, including you, and the furies, and me.

I thought how right now would be different if

we had just watered the lilacs, like we'd planned.

a gentle, nourishing.

in gentler, more nourishing times.

I saw you when you thought not, standing behind your purposely

stained glass window, colors blinding my eyes, you

winnowed me from behind.

leaving me out there with the earth breaking up under my feet.

MARCH 27th

strapped down in the on the

all white sheets, leather cuffed, handicapped, bruised,

stabbed.

I deep fried in the concrete block snake-pit,

watching one long light because of you who

I had loved.

I bled on the sheets from the stabbing, but no one came.

I was so ice ice ice cold. even in my head hot sweat.

shaking off, trying. shock.

I tried to push the silver pain you'd given me just

last night out into the, through the window, to the night lawn, but it

wouldn't go through the glass pane.

one spot somewhere else I fought thinly with my broken hand,

but it would not leave me alone because

I had loved you.

you had no idea, anymore.

MARCH 30th

the green soft Kleenex fills my wet hand.

poisoned by my un-whispered grief.

I see there is dust on the leaves of your plant, not all of which you see.

still has the store tag tied on a stem.

I keep my face away from you.

look out the small square window.

I have decided not to let you see me just about

to cry.

once your eyes looked out like eyes not looking just to see, but

eyes looking out to draw in and soothe.

not today.

the words I need most of all to say to you

I cannot get my lips to form.

GEORGIA BROWN'S GREAT ESCAPE

She was only a wisp, thin like toothpick trees, she always stood lost inside the pink and bright yellow housedresses she and her only daughter both wore.

they took in other's washed clothing to iron, make a little spending money, both irons pounding down in separate but next-door houses, each watching on the television the same soap operas so they could talk about them later in the evening.

I thought I had forgotten the noise of pounding irons, but I have not.

after her daughter and son-in-law adopted me, I took refuge from their cruelty, sometimes hiding in King's dog house, my arms hugging around his big collie neck. One day I found King dead, lying on his side in the yard. I knelt down and put my arms around him, gave him a kiss, Eileen said, don't do that—germs.

Fuck germs.

I wasn't sure if I liked Georgia Brown, she spoke Hungarian whenever she got mad, it was a language that scared me.

One sunny summer day when no wind sifted through the tree leaves, me and jack and eileen moved to another city, in another house, leaving Georgia behind with the silent wind and the buried King.

then I knew my mommy would never find me never again. I felt my guts go to my knees.

boxes and boxes of stuff I couldn't see what it was inside them, were carried by movers out of the house, then furniture and beds stuffed into trucks, I had seen that done before when my grandma and grandpa moved from one house to another.

I didn't know why people moved. all the rooms were in a different order than before. Smells were new and sometimes strange, and everything had to be put in new and unfamiliar places.

few years had passed, enough to let the back yard seed turn into grass and get the cyclone fence put up to close off all the yard. fence had a steely gaze on all sides, I didn't like it.

One fall day, as red and green leaves fell off the trees, giving up,

jack and eileen sold Georgia's house without any warning, she couldn't understand why. she cried and screamed Hungarian at them as they sold her antiques and threw out her dishes and silverware and tossed away her contentment and independence in separate boxes.

they moved her in with us. the scream-fests raged between Eileen and Georgia for weeks, but the thin wisp of my new grandma finally settled in, she spent most of the time in her bedroom writing in her diary, especially after jack yelled at her in the kitchen where she came out for her morning cup of coffee—two sugars, no cream. jack was mad 'cause Georgia watched his work boot feet come in, she didn't say good morning-boo-bastard-sip-shit to him at his arrival.

She didn't come out for morning coffee any of the days no more.

so Georgia loved her radio instead, playing loud the Cleveland Indians baseball games, she should have been in the stands, she rooted for and cursed the team she loved so loudly that Eileen told her to shut the hell up and took the radio away. she knew it was the last fun Georgia had.

Eileen read Georgia's diary, ripped out all the pages threw them in the black kitchen wastebasket, stomped back into the room like an army and slapped Georgia so hard she cried out.

I heard it from down on the floor behind my bedroom door, where I was kept in my own prison and I thought about King's dog house, dog always on a short chain, dog in prison, too.

the last uprising was when Georgia said Eileen treated me like an animal. Georgia never spoke again, she gave up, like the leaves and me and King, the battle was over, Eileen ruled us all.

Georgia Brown put her artillery away.

I was so lost and so sad, and so not understanding. me and her, we were just alike, I saw the just alike in her eyes when she was called out to eat dinner at the dining room table, where her only daughter portioned out the food on her mother's plate, and on my plate, and we could not ever think about asking for more, even if our bellies would hurt from hunger. we both knew Eileen shopped at the grocery store every Friday and bought a whole lot of food. cookies and eggs and bacon and cereal and cheese and bologna and olives and chocolate candies and crackers in the cupboard me and Georgia were not allowed to touch, but I touched the cheese once to see what would happen when Eileen went out the front door to get the mail out of the mailbox. nothing happened so I snatched a slice and scurried back into my room.

oh. the wonderful yellow soft cheese in my hands. so melty in my mouth even though I took the smallest bites to make it last longer. I thought about sneaking some to Georgia, but decided selfishly to keep it for myself—it slid down my throat so smoothly. someday I would steal more cheese.

Then.

oh, that day, it lives in my mind forever, so joyfully wonderful, I grabbed it and held on.

a Friday when eileen shopped, and jack slept in snoring cascades, I heard teeny little mouse steps, quick-creep down the hallway into the kitchen to the forbidden phone. Georgia calling for a cab to pick her up at the house!

oh my god, oh my god, oh my god, she's gonna get caught, she won't make it, the cab will take so long to come and Eileen will beat her back into her room, oh no, oh shit, I had to hold onto my breath, please come cab, cab come, or it will be too late

cab came.

Georgia Brown walked right out the front door, closing it quietly behind her, I heard the cab door slam, I heard the cab car drive away.

sweet, brave, thin, valiant, hungry, beaten Georgia Brown escaped.

Eileen did not rule us all any longer.

not even her great red fury when she found no Georgia Brown in her room

could still the, stay the, ruin the, take away the

Hope.

Hope

Swelling up inside me,

Making me tall enough to crack my very own

Shell of once helpless defeat, she.

Georgia Brown left her artillery all over the house in places only I could find
it.

WHERE THE SUN SHINES

the sun shines even here, light, dark shadows over mattress trash.
rusted trucks, shattered glass, grey dryers and sinks,
thrown toilets and shards, tin roofs in the woods.

the fields left long ago must squint and frown their way down to
the tiny river that belches pop cans and beer bottle caps,
it looks to me like it's become one long weeping green tear.

an old farm withered arm, a rotting wooden bridge just
slapped down, trapped. A doghouse on it's side, dog gone.

untrimmed trees shedding, happy bushes sprawling, ivy reaches out as if
to stake it's claim on everything it's arms can reach, untethered roses on
bushes
and daisies gone wild, waving in the agitated wind.

unoccupied, unvisited, unwanted, soon
the wild will repopulate, mice building family homes in broken
trucks. moles, voles, rats, feral cats, foreclosure dogs in packs

wondering, maybe, where their once warm homes have gone.
people loved them, then let them go, pushed them out of cars in
dangerous traffic, where they stood, not understanding.

fleas exercise their long hind legs hopping from mattress to dog
finding their freedom from once remembered chemicals to kill

them to keep them out and off.

I want to walk the place my feet in the river my feet on the land,
my head asleep on the farmhouse floor.

no cell phones no neighbors no watchers nor peepers nor teen-age slang.
no texting, computers, no ipods.

just me growing wild with the trash and the dogs and the roses,
at home with the unwanted, the betrayed, the forgotten, the lost--
the sun shines even here.

THE THIEF

some nights, as a ghost.

I tip toe to the basement below the attic.

I am looking for my artwork and my cat.

I watch a stranger come carry off all my alabaster.

and my wax. I only began to form them into the shapes of

those who were imaginary, but being a ghost, I cannot stop him.

he, thief, has my imagination now, my wax will melt in the thick

heat, which is why I could not sleep nor stay solid.

sculptures melting into woes I had not intended.

in the basement someone said my old, fat cat was pregnant,

I know she isn't, but I cannot get my legs up to go see. I was

only going to cut her toenails shorter, but I can't even find

my acrylic nuclear Madonna. her eyeball fell out.

cat creeps round the concrete corner, sly. she walks through

the middle of my legs and hisses.

I am not in my right form, she doesn't know me.

THE WRONG LIFE

he was rung awake by the wrong clock, it was not his bed.

went to work at the wrong job, couldn't get the unfamiliar work done.

he took it home, stayed up all night long counting one cent errors

time after futile time.

next day, when he took it in, the manager was mad.

fired him.

at his own job, they liked the wrong person who was now

doing his old job.

they would not give it back to him.

driving someone else's car, the GPS was broken.

it sent him into Idaho, but he carried the wrong token.

so he sat in someone else's house, in a chair in the wrong kitchen.

hoping someone would come in, and give him some direction.

to some other place.

when they came, they did not know him, made him leave by the back door.

he walked, bewildered, too far out into the road.

car driver's horns blasted him to get out of the way.

out of the way. the way out of.

he was the wrong person, living the wrong life,

the sidewalk would not lead him home.

THE LOVE I'D FOUND

I watched you bat the featherbed we furied all night long,

I loved you, loved you, then

because, dear god, I knew you were the love I'd found.

you put your arms around me by the kitchen sink as you

cooked us breakfast at noon, you loved to

cook. The aphrodisiac aromas filling us up, floating, of

spices, salted hissing bacon strips, over-easy eggs, sliced from a fresh loaf
toast.

we chose a fine red wine, whitefish to be battered in corn starch later,

with pepper and salt and the love, the love I'd found.

I treasured every breath I dared allow myself to breath, I

read, re-read, inhaling every card, letter you wrote me, sent.

words and words of love and joy, longing, missing, hand drawn kissings.

I jumped up and up and up

inside without ever coming down, because you, dear god, you

were -you -were -you -were -the never ending, all consuming, planning-

our -futures -together so we'd never be apart love.

Love I'd found.

you said April. I agreed. April was a wonderful start spring month to move,

I sat home, packing all the boxes in my mind, what to leave out what to leave behind, what to hang in your closet with yours, to place in your kitchen as mine

Ours.

contentment complete as Paris, the finch, perched on his swing, in his cage and

sang us songs about the love we'd found.

we laughed at your friends who said we wouldn't make it, kissing on the couch

in your brother's living room, he said we would not last the year, but

my brother didn't say that, said he liked you a lot, even though he got scared

trying to find his lost way back home, and my friends were happy for me,

smiling at the joy they could see in my heart, the love I had found made

multi-colored softness, seen as an aura, Tom said, around the shape of my head.

and Tom knew everything about auras, all that could be known.

but

I never.

packed. my moving boxes.

they laid funny flat on my living room floor.

I bought Boone's Farm fruity something god-awful to shut up the scream in my soul the scream.

in.

my soul.

I treasured each awful aching breath I could barely it hurt so hard breathe because.

dear god.

you.

were.

the love.

I'd found

THE ROLLING CAN

the small man has a reputation.

he is the freeway flasher and

he pees against the grocery wall.

there is no sympathetic helper agency.

welfare workers eye him with disgust and suspicion.

wearing his green and dirty coat from the army,

once.

he was a soldier.

not now.

one shoe sole is tied onto the top of his foot,

long matted unkempt hair hangs to his shoulder tops.

because it is their job, the welfare workers call

whosit and them, to know what they are officially allowed to do

without violating some small print regulation.

they do not notice what he needs.

newer clothes, different shoes, a bath, a blanket.

he stands self conscious, hands in his pants pocket

his reputation between thumb and right forefinger.

he gets a bag of groceries in a used brown paper bag.

a stale loaf of bread, Campbell's in cans, dry milk, some coffee.

an agency van driver drops him off at the corner of a bad neighborhood block

where, a few buildings down, he walks to his rented room in a tilting house.

along the way one soup can rubs a fuzzy hole in the brown bag corner,

it rolls along the sidewalk, bouncing up over uneven sidewalk slabs.

with no free hand, he desperately bends over

picks it up.

holding it tight, while pressing the torn now bag held from the bottom

so hard, as if it were a thing holy, sacredly against his chest.

THE TWENTIETH NUDE

so this.

is the twentieth nude.

the best yet.

a moody willow on a green spring day

by light dancing. daring to bare all.

I flee from that frame.

could be

her dancing calls the feeling that I'm moving

in cylindrical and recti-linear norms to even space.

collapse my form.

I knew this feeling long before today.

before this nude.

I sat in an ochre jacket and

had a longing for your presence, intensely for your presence

insanely for your presence, and

you didn't come and you didn't come and

when you did you saw.

my state of twisted up undone.

your nude will never understand that.

she reminds me that I am

still am

losing grace.

THE LINK

among the living things I see a connection I

can only partly fathom. it

links each one of us to every other one

of all species and kind.

the fish I keep and feed is a reminder of

our long ago watery past. the cats I keep as pets were once

bigger, free and wild.

 my dog, the wolf. linked to packs.

the ferrets,

small innocents,

linked to time after the

fall of mighty dinosaurs, those.

who fell in great heaps of hungry death

only wanting green things or others to eat. even

that mass extinction connects us, those

who ruin and pillage the earth, wanting

more condos and malls and laundromats. we

who so long for connection in our every and everyday lives,

keep on breaking it all up

with bulldozers, buildings, shovels. super highways.

breaking it up.

breaking it up.

link by

link by

link.

road kill rot is usual, blood and brains squashed out

while crows, others, feed and fly between cars.

Maurice complained about the deer eating his green things

off his back forty, said it was alright to kill a lot of deer, as

they were not native to this country.

neither were we.

knowing that no argument was possible.

it is often just not. possible.

we place safer deer of ceramic, plastic, just so. around the garden.

no one cares about

the link, it.

does not waver or wobble, it.

runs from point to point to point through

all the times and universes it. runs.

to and right through God.

STARVATION ON THE DINING ROOM FLOOR

I thought about it.

was it better to sit on the floor in a posed position, not

allowed to move an inch, or to be tied to my red toddler chair?

one time I stepped on the dog's foot by accident, trying to sneak

into the kitchen for food and even though he yelped and got me caught

I decided it was better to sit on the dining room floor.

I could sneak.

but not step on the dog's foot ever again.

on the fourth day, when I was four,

Eileen asked Jack if he thought they should feed me dinner.

no.

Eileen objected. she said they had to feed me sometime, but.

Jack had the best idea in the whole world. he said go ahead.

fill her plate with food, call her to the table, and she can watch me eat it.

all up. all gone.

the red pain in my stomach burned with hunger, pulsing.

a pink wet empty void.

later, after dinner was finished.

Jack.

offered me a piece of chocolate from the candy plate.

as I reached for one, he pulled the plate away and gave me

a really good kick in the stomach.

but.

I

fooled them.

I had lots of stuff to eat when they weren't looking.

I chewed all the toes and fingers off Tiny Tears, she would just

have to hobble through life when she learned to walk.

I chewed off all the corners of all my wood blocks, I even

chewed off my own fingernails, and found the best, biggest

dust balls under the dining room table.

I wondered if my blocks would still stack up on top

each other when I wanted to make a tower,

with their corners being gone.

sawdust in my belly.

TOOTH FAIRY

baby teeth of mine moved loose to

make the way for big people's teeth underneath, hiding

in my gums.

my mommy told me long ago about the tooth fairy. she

said when you have a loose tooth, you have to put it under your pillow

so the tooth fairy can find it and leave you a coin.

maybe only one, maybe more.

I remembered.

I was excited when my front tooth was moving loose, maybe

I would get a dime, or even better, a whole quarter!

but.

Eileen said

no.

she dragged me down into the basement.

I notice she has a big butt.

she finds Jack's red handled pliers, comes sits on me. pulls,

rips my tooth out and throws it carelessly into the trash can as

I bleed on the press and stick floor. she says the tooth fairy

doesn't want my teeth.

I think Eileen is the tooth fairy's evil sister.

BLUELIGHT

I had devolved to scentlessness.

no odor, foul or posied exuded from my being.

what it meant to be me, as I spit on the ground into a witless dust,

was to be half-dead to everything, still bathe on a regular basis.

I kept telling myself.

telling myself I did not mind it, and bought towels on sale at K-Mart.

I wasn't quite convincing as I hungered. wanting

things past known.

hugging someone, holding on. and

the things waiting on my doorstep, unacknowledged.

things I knew I did not want were plentiful.

the barren nights, the liquid ones

which felt like wet blood, carrying me far down

through the avenues of my nightmares, it

always smelled like drowning.

now.

the towels are tiny threads I can see through

and not that much has changed.

I sometimes long for one night of starry sky,

rounded moon,

gentle breeze.

I dream of becoming.

I dream of becoming the scent of

an autumn pre-dawn morning.

KILLING EACH OTHER

1.

they always said it.

behind my back and to my face.

if they could kill and bury me,

they would.

almost.

too close.

the long filet knife held to my throat

while his hands held me close and so tight.

I thought about the two of them digging

my grave out quickly in a no whisper woods.

2.

I often thought about killing them both.

somehow.

almost .

too close.

when I took his rifle down and loaded it.

drag their corpses up into the car trunk

and drive them away in the night.

right up to the hot coals, devil waiting gates of Hell.

HOMELESS

sat inside the stairwell, stiff with February blizzard.

sing-song. sing along. rolling

tiny snowballs make music in my brain.

I am homeless and free.

homeless and free,

does anybody want to be homeless like me?

silly song stopped my thinking about where to sleep tonight.

not here on the stair steps, I'd get accordion back. so scared the man or woman who lived

in the upstairs apartment would come in. or out.

see me smoking cigarettes

homeless and free.

homeless and free,

does anybody want to be homeless like me?

could sleep in unlocked cars. can

sleep in the closed end alley, all

wrapped around in my wonderful filthy pink carpet

I had found in the dumpster by Kippy's diner.

tomorrow,

I will jump a slow train,

railroad tracks a few blocks away.

I will go to Florida,

sit in the sand

sit in the sun

wade in the ocean waters

never be hungry again,

eat the bananas and coconuts.

spear the fish.

someone could teach me how.

I would find a guitar, sing songs

for smoke and coffee money

not to tell anyone I was just sixteen, and

homeless and free.

does anybody want to be homeless like me?

my thinking brain stood in front of me, dressed like me, angry.

furious, with chapped cheeks and cracked hand skin, told me

stop it stop. stupid sing-song. look at all these cars outside. going

home to hot dinners and warm bed sheets. I hate them. It's not fair.

why does one choice to elude a certain death have to lead me into this, this.

another place where I need to elude death?

gonna spend my money, freeze

myself dead and no one will know, and

think about this while you sit smoke and sing.

no one will care.

go away.

I prefer my daydream, and my sing-song.

I might meet hobos when I hop the slow train,

dangerous men people talked about in whispers, they

jumped on slow trains all the time. maybe,

maybe they would lend me gloves for a while, they were

homeless like me.

homeless and free.

wondering which way was Florida from here, as I decided

I did not like menthols.

they were cold in my mouth,

could maybe make me freeze faster.

which way, which way. which way

to get to warm Florida fast?

south dummy.

FALLEN ANGEL

while I dreamed of hell last night, I

never felt the flames, but other people I

did not know stood in a group away from me, whispering.

in louder voices they were speaking with the devil, that sadly

fallen angel who had once known heaven.

he came to me during intermission, opened up the door to hell

for me to see. I trembled with such agony, it was the doorway to

the madness I had fought always. his darkened face smiled almost

tenderly, he told me he would come back later to discuss with

me the other things. walked away pouring coffee into his

cup from a white carafe. left alone,

I dropped a pebble down the door into hell, causing screaming I

shrunk from, woke up in darkness from. walking clumsily,

I held my head, held a heated

stone in my hand. holding darkness so hard

I slammed my head against the door frame.

IT WASN'T MOZART

woman called me out of class.

said go to room #214

music room.

maybe someone wanted me to play the forbidden piano.

a thin-haired woman was sitting in the empty room at Mr. Wagner's desk.

oh.

not Mozart.

a social worker from the Children's Home instead.

so many complaints, she said.

soft-spoken, she seemed kind.

tell me, she said.

tell.

I sat in yellow silence in the cracked brown chair, and

I did not know how to tell.

I blurted, I babbled, I tried not

to blubber over the top of the tear trails serenading my thin ghost face.

beatings.

bad ones.

losing conscious ones.

Jack, rape sex, bad man.

Eileen tortures, she thinks it is funny, and

it makes her so happy.

one meal a day hunger for always, can

you take me away with you?

she needs to make a home visit, first.

can you take me away then?

they are going to kill me one day.

maybe,

don't know.

policy procedure paperwork.

can't make promises.

hands tied.

oh.

no.

don't go there then.

no home visit.

they will beat me when you leave, if you leave me there.

sorry.

I can't allow it.

my hands tied too.

MY FATHER'S SHOES

I never saw my father's shoes.

he never wore sneakers, he was from a practically ancient generation of

farmers who swore and smoked a lot out in the barn to get the hell away

from their fat and diabetic wives cooking dinner in the house.

the only shoes I ever really looked at were the flip flops he wore over

his socks the night before he died. he said his shoes, the ones I never saw,

would not fit over his swollen feet.

we went to dinner at the diner. dad ordered soup he did not slurp up sloppy.

that was his way of eating soup, although he told us not to eat it that way.

then ordered banana cream pie for dessert, picked up his fork, put it back down.

stared at the fork, stared.

stared at the white and yellow pie slice, finally handed it to me.

maybe when his feet swelled up, his throat swelled up, too.

I forked food off Tom's plate, as I always did, knowing dad would look at me,

angry, and angrily, try to say something that never came out of his mouth.

at home, he always slammed the cupboard doors when he was angry, or

pounded his clenched fists on the counter top, wearing his mad shoes.

he died the next morning, after bringing in the Sunday paper. his emphysema stopped

his breathing. no more hacking and spitting out snot stuff that stuck to Tom's car

like a glue as we were, I was, speeding down the highway

miles over the speed limit. it scared him. made him cough more.

his dentures got stuck in his throat. Tom found him, cold and blue. I
wondered what shoes he was wearing, even though he was in bed.

and how dead.

People who wear dentures need to take them off at night, float them in a

bottle or a can or a jug or a jar with blue denture stuff. he certainly didn't
need

his dentures to get the Sunday paper, although he might have needed his
shoes.

emphysema causes breathlessness, and the last time I saw him, he was not
breathing.

he was two days dead, his body hard and stiff. we did not bring him any
shoes to

wear, as he was being cremated, didn't want any shoe laces in his ashes.

when I knocked on his hard shoulder, it felt like knocking on a door,

maybe in the crematory, he would throw off flames filled with the odor,

say, of pine or cedar.

then.

coals.

ashes.

I own a picture of my father, taken when he was very young and in the
Marines.

He's stuffed into his uniform, belt tight, not smiling. came straight from the
taxidermist,

so no room to breathe in those clothes.

BASEMENT MEMORY

I am lost and lost, finally given up

for dead.

and though I don't wish it to happen,

it does.

bones start poking through drying skin and

snap off.

I am becoming dust for someone I don't know

to sweep up in a bin, a basket,

a brown bag.

a barrel. in the basement, I search so despicably desperate,

for a can , a crock, a candle I could make fire from

the breath

of the furnace flame. but my eyes have fallen out.

if only I could find them on this dit-dot floor, I could.

I would.

renew. if I could renew, I could live again, but not

like before.

living like dancing and singing and weeping and joy, all

the way past the memories of in the basement

poking bones.

BLANCHE'S MOTHER

I wondered why,

as I poured blue bowl cleaner into a badly limed toilet,

how I can so effortlessly continue to breathe when I

stopped caring about it long ago. the intake of oxygen and its'

pollutants, the exhalation of carbon dioxide and some atoms of

last night's dinner.

Blanche's mother was delighted with her continuing breathing.

at age 97 she sat on the floral patterned couch, her old woman's stomach

hard, pushed out in front of her like a pregnancy.

she told me, " I still kicking." as if I'd be delighted with her breathing, too.

Two weeks later, she dropped dead on her worn linoleum kitchen floor.

Blanche displayed non-dismay when her mother's Polish synapses stopped.

"This comes to everyone." she told me, as if it were one of her old lesson plans

she'd pulled out just for this occasion. said you must be strong and set an

example for your family.

but I had no family at that time. I knew that I

would not need to be strong for anyone.

FOR MARY ANNE

wondering about the inside minds of child molesters

has been a futile wandering.

what

when

why

is it?

the perverted thoughts enter their minds,

eventually hardened into decision.

violent action acted on.

how is it decided when will be the first time, the first child?

personal privacy unspeakably,

it is said,

lost and torn away.

ripped and taken.

long twisted trails always running into knots tied up.

sadly and helplessly I cast long thoughts, pointless ones.

netlike thoughts cast out for

all the children through all times and all the ages.

who have been broken.

down and up.

turned inside out.

most in settings of normalcy

a certainty.

"don't tell."

babies, toddler, teens.

some die.

like the four month old baby who's mother held her down.

others manage, in tangles and mangles with tentacles to grow into madness, denial, repression,

disassociation.

always.

there is not one who never minds.

on the evening news,

in magazine articles,

once or twice on talk shows on the television, but not that often.

it is told of.

stories are told.

most are never.

known.

always, people do not want to hear it.

no.

put it away.

banish it.

it did not happen,

I know him, and

he is a nice man.

he would never.

I know ones.

I know

Donell.

Patti .

Vic.

Susie.

and Mary Anne.

his niece.

she was Bernie's mother, and with

cracked anguish, consumed by cancer cells,

she still cried to Beth

when she told,

after all the years and years had passed,

she was forever damaged by his evil.

must be an evil.

must be.

Linda thought Susie was a whore.

but when I told her what had happened,

because I knew, she reflected long,

remembering those times next door when something did not seem

to be right after Susie and her rabbit on a leash

returned and were untypically silent.

silent. "you should have told me."

I never had the chance.

"does Ray know?"

no, he did not,

should have.

most likely did,

most likely denied his neighbor knowledge.

she decided it explained a lot of behaviors, was going to think about how to forgive her.

no thinking needs to be involved.

Donell is dead to it, she will never let it out, or in.

Vic.

death is not punishment enough.

death happens to everyone

pervert or not.

perhaps not to die, but to be

buried alive and conscious of being slowly eaten

by a monster I can't see or name.

slimy, with little needle sharp teeth the eating slowly, ever so.

thousands and thousands of years of it.

sad Mary Anne.

his niece.

crying with remembrance of the little girl of four she had once been.

maybe death will bring peace to her

erase her fourth year.

even if that could happen,

I am the one who cannot find peace.

cannot forget her life's long pain, I

will remember it on and on.

I cannot forgive

about the pain.

is there punishment waiting for me,

who cannot forgive?

I will accept it.

embrace it.

welcome it.

long for it.

make it last.

BELL NIGHT

Bruce loud on the jukebox, bar crowded into smoke-filled air,

if you could call it air, it was the only thing we had to breathe into and out

of our lungs. People packed, pawing and pushing against me, I cupped my

hands around my mouth, shouted out to Nancy, get us a table somewhere.

She had no gloves, she drove around town with socks on her hands to pick
me up in her heatless volkswagon beetle. it was red and rusty.

I had gloves. had no boots or socks to keep my feet warm, though.

I kept thumping them on the car floor to keep what I imagined to be

circulation circulating. we'd played pool earlier at the Blind Owl, stoned. I
put my quarter in the slot and

ran the table, wondering why I could not feel the focus, see the clarity and
linear in undrugged life. asked Nancy what she thought about that,
whatever she told me was plucked

out of her mouth by the long, quick cold hands of winter wind.

I saw her mouth move, forming words unfathomed in the frozen downtown
night light. finally. sitting at the table Nancy found, I said to hell with pre-
med, I needed to save myself instead of others , besides. I always got so far
behind in algebra class.

Nancy said to find a tutor.

we drank the introductory shot of schnaaps, maybe I would find a tutor in
the bottom of one of our pitchers of beer. the sudden secret understanding
of all mathematics, linear and clear, no more of that halting, only half
understanding .

we won pitchers of beer two times that night when the bar bell was rung,
how could we be happier, luckier, drunker? Nancy firmly believed I would
never find my family, she said it

never happens. sad and angry for a moment, I pounded on the closed restroom door.

someone said "In a minute." I would pee out my pitchers possibly now, pee puddles all over the bar floor, anyone would think it was spilled beer. same color, same texture, no froth. fine. I would keep my agony over the damned impossible to myself, and drop out of algebra again, take up social studies and history. Nancy pointed out that I would never find a job in any of those fields, so I poured another glass of beer and pondered.

how was it possible for her to always be so certain and confident? such an ongoing optimist using words like "never" to me. I didn't tell her about the hope slivers

I injected myself with daily, she would have smiled and told me that she read an article about how the research concluded hope injections don't work, especially in sliver form. never.

Maybe they don't work.

never.

work.

but it was Nancy's never,

not mine.

I kept them hidden in the medicine cabinet over my white and silver bathroom sink,

in an old Tums bottle and I would keep using them. Nancy sloppily said, smiling, and merrily drunk, that I would never get my memories validated.

I was drunk, too, but.

I don't, didn't, know why she thought it was all so funny.

wearing socks on her hands, now that was funny.

DONNER

train wheels had replaced all the gears in my brain,

stopped.

I pretended not to see you waiting so as to study

you from the corner of my eye.

time has slippered feet but still it

leaves images.

I did not know you.

your eyes were brightly excited,

your welcoming smile warm,

the vodka before the talking,

before bed.

necessary.

the tennis before the snowstorm

surprising.

the anchovies in New York City

salty.

the things that are held like

fragile tiffany.

JUDY

mostly

I remember about the wine.

red wine.

it came in glasses and bottles and jugs and barrels.

always there.

in the refrigerator, on the table, the countertop.

sometimes

I remember the charcoal penciled barn

you framed and hung, even though it was still spotted

with Freddie's pancake syrup.

in the summer

in the yard

I ran with the children hanging onto my back

while you stood there,

sipping wine.

THE BIGGEST CHRISTMAS SURPRISE

Christmas!

Christmas Morning!

Threw back the unwanted covers, ran down the long stairway in

My pink feet pajamas, ran into the living room to see

What toys Santa had brought me.

but.

brought me nothing.

i walked all around the tree in case he hid them.

no.

Wait!

A red white stocking hanging from the fireplace

For me!

There WAS a present—something big all the way down in the toe, I

Reached all the way down and,and,and

pulled out a lump of coal.

"Look at the bundle of switches Santy left by the fire-place."

oh.

"You were very bad this year. Very bad. How do you like your lump of coal?

maybe we can use it in the fireplace."

five year old tears washed clean my five year old face,

looking back at the two of them they were smiling.

I cried

damage not to be undone.

heart broken.

A long long time later I heard them go into the laundry room and out,

They carried armfuls of presents in, setting them down in front of the tree.

some for me, wrapped in pretty bows and shiny snowman paper.

but.

I didn't want them

anymore.

THE HUNTING

certifiably insane

because

I hunt you in these bars each Friday night, I

know you could be here, I'd get a glimpse, a glance.

you might care. I told you I liked your shirt in history class and

you and Sam made fun of Cat Stevens. I sit and buy these and these glasses

of half bad draft because of you. you will never know it.

something such vitality in your tousled hair you wear out drinking.

electricity tingling in a wire, a sauna warm fire. the ball game, the

fireworks. the night of Roxy music, cramming for history of

the medieval and monks I said ate yogurt in the desert while wearing

hair shirts.

they could have.

I only saw you flex intentional emotion eyes once

when you shared what you began there. quick sighs breathed by

the corner of your breaking veneer black desk, and.

the rainy day offer of one crying shoulder I refused, the bar night stabbed

by your eventually expressive lit red cigarette, if

you knew I came here you might laugh your orange spherical laugh

and I would have to store back these images forever.

what you began here.

FINDING FREEDOM IN OUTER SPACE

true too blue sky

grass grows green, unmowed, in a forever field.

heavy yellow sun hurts my dreamy eyes, I just then know I'm not alone,

look quickly over my shoulder. I see her far away and for

a moment, I feel safer. she cannot catch me from far away.

I do wonder, however, how it is possible, in God's grace, for such

an Eileen evil to exist on such a perfect day. I left her long ago, but

she keeps coming to me in my daydreams and nightdreams.

something shoosh sails beside me and on, it seems to be a red, sharp shape

circle. I look back, see her throwing out, with the grace of a magician, blue triangles,

more red circles, yellow rectangles, all with a life in them, their aim to cut me,

make me stop to bleed. racing across the wonderfully grassy field in tip top

ways geometric shapes usually defy.

it is a spell, woven by her liver spotted hands, to make me jump, dodge, slip behind trees.

lose ground.

lose all ground.

standing so suddenly on the last grass, before the great beyond, the very edge

of the end of the world.

behind me. Eileen starts to smile in triumph.

closer.

coming closer.

her claws reach out from strangely elongated arms, but

I jumped.

I jumped into the stars, the stasis,

the wonder and the awe, my body arched,

my arms outstretched into.

wings.

the evil Eileen stood back there, bewildered.

she would never jump,

so afraid of her feet leaving solid ground.

THE MEANING OF HARRY

I asked him what he thought of me when I lived alone on Lincoln

he said he thought I was crazy.

but I wasn't.

ever

crazy.

Harry's empathy had been pretended.

later,

when we walked the shaded park path, he told me about Jane.

she was crazy, he said.

and he didn't know what to do with her.

do with her.

later,

I met Jane.

told her what Harry had said about me, about her.

but Jane was all right now, her slit wrists were healing

and the slit waterbed was dry.

she was in therapy now.

sleeping in another place without a bed.

Harry's love for her had been only thin.

Harry thought of himself as very Zen.

bought all his food at the Kent Natural Food store

and let his beard grow a little longer to enhance his imagined aura.

took philosophy classes, consumed the classics, thinking that

such absorption made him a wise man.

it did not.

when I asked him what he thought of Aristotle, he

could not answer.

he did not listen to the world he lived in.

I let him go, I let go of him

when we met in the art building.

TWO CATS, TWIN GIRLS

first.

two white long-haired kittens with sky blue eyes.

I remember.

I have pictures of them.

one is sitting on my windowsill in the bedroom.

I do not remember that.

all the days and all the nights

they were chained with leashes, one each

to the bottom bed posts of

my bed.

cat box stuffed between them on the floor.

Eileen tortured them.

she kicked them, choked them, took food and water away.

one day the fun was gone and the cats gone.

maybe she killed them.

I know they were beautiful.

I know Eileen damaged the rest of their lives.

if they had lives left.

then.

years on.

in the foster home on Patterson, they had their own kids

and Skippy, and those six year old twin girls, me.

Sarah and Emily.

I saw them sitting on the couch day after endless day,

tied together with a kind of home-made harness

like oxen in a yoke.

they were forbidden to speak.

I looked at them when I walked through the living room to

get a cold drink, sweating from paint-scraping.

it was too much to bear.

it had nothing to do with me.

night after night I heard them cry when foster mother took them upstairs

to their bedroom. foster mother has no name.

one day

when I couldn't take it

take it

take it

any longer.

I told my social worker about the twins, how she treated them.

social worker did not listen.

said these people had been very good foster parents for a long time,

and if the girls were punished, there must be a reason for it.

there was no reason for it.

no reason.

but meanness I knew well and had seen so much of before.

they were innocents.

foster mother was taking away the life in them.

wished I could knock her head against the porch wall.

then run in, free them, set them free.

stunned.

aching for them, not able to do anything, so

I didn't go back that night.

didn't want to hear screaming and crying twin girls.

stayed out with Tom and Reba at Kevin's house.

we gleefully drank many quarts of Mad Dog,

skinny-dipped in old man Johnson's home-made pond.

threw stones at his ducks and his dog.

THE TUNNEL

dad was dead in Dade county.

he told me about it much later, looking stricken.

he said it was only for a minute, and they wouldn't let him have his

dentures after they rebooted him.

he whispered about the tunnel he could not talk about, it was, he said,

the tunnel of death. he could hear the people on the floor above him,

so he pounded on the ceiling, but no light, the tunnel was the blackest
black.

he stepped over, stumbled around in the tunnel, looking for a

Marlboro, waiting for the train that came and went and

left him, he said, so sadly, he tried to get on but they would not

let him in, they asked him for his ticket, but he did not have one.

that is when, he said, down there in the darkness alone, he knew

that he was in hell. someone he did not see told him the others would

join him later on, and they would all march down together.

no, dad.

I said, to reassure him, as if I knew all about it.

WEATHERFRIEND

tell it to your weatherfriend

the moon has cast a spell

from April to November 17th.

and in the city streets, they say

a dog ate Horatio Alger,

a meal that rotted all its' teeth.

tell him that the lakes have dried.

the reservoirs are low. dead fish

spit out on beaches edges,

while white dandelions will, for nothing, blow away.

when the spell is over, we

don't know what to expect. we

sit around, amongst each other and wonder

what comes next .

a time to plant, a time to weep?

ask what he can do.

icy lakebeds under stars give

no chance for renewal.

tell it to your weatherfriend

the moon has cast a spell

from April to November 17th.

when you tell about the spell

will you

make him see and know

unbearable dreams have fallowed.

are being thrown deep in a well.

NICHOLAS

once upon a time, I told Nick, watching his small eyes widen,

and in a land far away, there lived a purple yak.

"with feet?"

yes, I continued. the yak had 14 feet, and he lived in the land of lotus eaters.

"what's a lotus eater?"

a lotus eater, I explained, is an animal, who eats giant

red flowers, and the flowers have magical properties.

"what's a poperty?"

property. property is land . it is stuff that belongs to people. daddy might say,

"These tools are my property."

a realtor might say, "This land is my property."

a lotus would say," Magic is one of my properties."

I knew to get out of properties. so I redirected his attention to the lotus eaters and

purple yak. The purple yak, had one shoe for each foot, and

none of it's shoes matched so.

one day, while walking down the mountain to get a morning cup of water, the yak

fell over its' fourteen feet and landed in the deep pool by the mountains.

"Then what happened?" he asked.

Nothing.

"Nothing happens?"

Nope. nothing. it is the very end.

Nick said he didn't like the story, I

asked him why.

"Because the yak had too many feet and fell down the mountain into a pile
of boogers"!

his young child laughter at his own made-up ending

his wonderfully giggling, laughing.

It was an unmatchable sound, the happy laugh of a happy child.

each day we began the same way.

me and my cup of coffee,

he with his sippy- cup of juice.

out the front door, sit down on the single step,

our story telling stoop.

I told him the silliest stories pulled out, up. on the spot.

when Nicholas had a story for me

he'd forget the stoop, the step. he'd fly around the yard, arms out-

stretched, he was an airplane or giant bird. with his air rifle,

he was a cowboy riding a blue horse. in the army he was Joe.

to show me, he

jumped up on the picnic table bench.

he was a rabbit, a kangaroo, a horned toad.

fantastic adventures of tigers, thoughts of

his orange goldfish, the blackest , giantest bears in the woods,

all the while wielding his fallen tree branch for emphasis.

I listened.

watched his happiness.

amazed at the reach of his imagination.

self confidence was, is.

a lucky child's

greatest gift.

SGT. BRELO

After we fought about something that was nothing, he
motorcycled home black helmet protecting him. No such respite when his
father screamed at him for doing something that was nothing--like
continuing to be a failure in his eyes.

David didn't argue, because he stopped just long enough to go back to
the jungles of Vietnam. He ran to his room like an army under fire to get his
sweet cold pistol from his underwear drawer so he could kill them and not
be killed first, to
not lie dying on a soft Cong floor alone.

(he said he was so afraid of dying during his 2 years there).

When his brother burst into the room to take the pistol to stop a murder,
David
so afraid of dying, pistol whipped him to the floor, screaming "GOOK!".
Blood all over the bedroom floor in puddles, in spatters on the wall soaking
into
The soft blue Cong carpet.

I wasn't there, but felt I could have been--visualizing each shot frame by
frame, losing the lost, paying the cost, over and over again for all time, all
talk and action misunderstood, no one to protest to as

his brother's head was shaved in the local ER by Cong doctors who sewed
twenty seven black head
thread stitches and asked him if he saw the lights.

THE EMBER

savoring a time like a taste on my tongue.

remnants had been torn, but I gripped them hard, I

did not want to lose them.

me and mom eating cheerios out of a box in a motel room.

without milk.

my blue rabbit, I dragged him around by the ears, he

got dirty, but mommy washed him.

mom's watching me ride the mighty kiddie roller coaster

at the amusement park, then she holds me under my arms in the dead fish
creek

to keep my head above the water yellowed by sunshine.

the everlasting ember.

indestructible in the great long emptiness of Jack and Eileen years.

somewhere in the universe.

in a house under the night stars,

my mother was brushing her teeth by the bathroom sink

and night time mirror on the wall.

cooking dinner, washing dishes with her own sack full of memories of me.

my imperfect, sad, lonely mom.

she saved my life.

I would have to tell her.

she left me memories of a time when life did not hurt,

and love given from the heart was lasting and bonding and good.

I did not know where I would start.

but.

I would scrub down time and find.

Jo Anne.

THE SILENCE OF MARIE LEVEAU

New Orleans, St. Louis cemetery NO 1
I drew 3 X's with red chalk on the side of the high priestess's tomb,
then knocked on it 3 times.

legend said that by doing those 2 things at the same time, Marie
would wake up from her long dead death and grant your wish.
It could be so.
legends start somewhere with a small truth.
I pressed my body up against her tomb wall, listening
for, I don't know.
the sounds of fresh coffee or chicory brewing.

Help me.
I whispered.
There is no one who wants to hear about my screaming.
It hurts my ears.
Can you make it stop?

There was no sound, and no feeling of an answer.
I had hoped,
against my usual sense of and belief in reason.

slowly, I made sure I walked softly amongst the other dead in their vaults,
thinking that I might. that I should.
take my tiny sack of hope and maybe out of my jeans pocket and
lie it there on the ground,
a cemetery being a good place.

RAIN

they said a rain would come by seven.

some

drops blew in through the open window

with

greetings from my yellow curtains.

they fall and splash and wet the bed.

the winds came after.

they howled around the house

like a tribe of banshees.

the raindrops angrily fell harder,

smashing themselves below the sky

they.

die on black wet pavement.

HOLY CROSS

the ghost of my mother sat alone in the yielding wind

on the worn wooden bench. staring to the white stone cross.

I was not surprised to see her there, although I could not any longer

hold her see-through hand.

we had once often come to this holy outdoor shrine, she found a peace,

contentment, comfort there and needed to share it with me.

just me.

Tom came once, maybe more, to meet the sharing which had always all

his life eluded him, to see the icons of a faith we did not follow.

sitting there beside her I absorbed the other-worldly atoms of her energy,

still vibrant, near vivid. alive she had been in awe of me.

I did not deserve it.

I came for Mary, mother of God, and found mine.

A COCKROACH AND LARRY

Tim sat back in the broken blue chair with a cold beer

to relax after a hot construction work day.

he only saw the cockroach because the t.v. was broken.

it was as big as a bean, any damn bean, with those

antennae waving things on its' head crawling out of

a hole in the living room wall.

Tim decided to paste the bastards up in there with a roll of old

green-gray wallpaper left over from a job in the Heights.

he soaked it in the tub, he papered the living room and half-way

down the hall. it was the ugliest color.

washed up, hurried out to meet his room-mate Larry at a bar.

next morning Larry jumped in the tub to shower, slid head forward

on the wallpaper paste not scrubbed out and broke his jaw.

Tim told me Larry's jaw was wired shut for weeks and he had to drink

all his meals from Tim's red crazy straw.

mostly mashed up Ben and Jerry's ice cream.

the sounds that came out of Larry's wired jaw sounded latin and demonic,

his tongue trapped inside his mouth, couldn't get his sentences out.

all Larry wanted to say was, "that was some fall." and

"Tim, you son-of-a-bitch, I oughta kill you."

but Tim thought he said, "I don't want it all."

and took the food away.

me and mom and Tim laughed till our guts griped over that.

Larry didn't.

the roaches are trapped for now, heads sticking to fresh

wallpaper paste.

them being bugs,

not understanding.

MEETING JO ANNE

during the longest night, there was no need for sleep and my

heart pumped the purest joy. there was no need for blood, there was no
room for blood,

I may never need it again.

through the frosting window I watched the greatest, softest, most magical
snowflakes,

they were for me, for me, and in no hurry to reach the ground,

to an overture of their own they floated happily on the gentle night wind.

had to play Janis Ian's lullaby over and over again, eating each word,

paced, hands stuffed, pushed all the way down in both blue jean

pockets. stared intently and even fiercely into my bathroom mirror

every ten seconds, to re-study the features on my face trying frantically

to remember if I really resembled myself, or if the mirror was mistaken.

I did not count the minutes, because they were longest ones, allowing me to
more

completely absorb rapture so

always held small, stuffed long ago into only one cell so no one would ever
see it,

or find it or hurt it or use it or kill it with a gun I think I might have died else.

drove through the fallen unplowed snow in the early morning to Brady's,
where I took my coffee

and cream stick to the well worn comfort of the upstairs. I wanted to smile inside without being seen.

I stared at my pastry lying innocently on a white dish, and wondered if I could pull out

long ago love and stir it around in my coffee.

I found the house.

there it was, as it had always been, waiting for me. drove

up or down the long driveway, can't remember, it was gravel.

snow-laden silver maples smiled at me, nodding the way and,

I watched the deliberation of turning off the car with a car key and getting out.

of the car by car door.

and walking up the swept porch stairs.

my inadequate shoes making inadequate shoe noises

oh.

she had been waiting too.

she was opening the porch screen door for me, she

stopped me with her eyes, searching my face to see if it was really me and not

someone else playing a joke on her. I fell into her arms and held on tight, she

hugged me so hard I knew I could have stayed inside her embrace forever and

it would have been right and divine. celestial and should be.

my mother.

my long ago lost Jo Anne.

GREEK HISTORY FINAL

another pot of coffee black

into 4003. Greek history final.

studying at the student center at

a round white table, my books and papers spread out.

others, too. looking tired

walking by me with books under their arms.

four –thirty in the morning at Eunomia again.

kouros have chitons on and by

the time I get to Mycenae,

the Aeolics are gone.

my pen rolled off under the table.

my head froze up. I sit, watch the pen roll.

smoke.

sip hot coffe.

sail out and away.

if I could go to Mycenae,

I'd advise them not to take up space in Greek history books.

I could sell the kouros Levi jeans, explaining how durable they were.

they could use their chitons for pillowcases.

what if I screw it up and write the wrong blue book essay?

the one of my daydreaming.

Lycurgus walks right out of here and grows

a snaky tail, heading , head down,

for a Spartan road.

they will kill him there,

because and Circle A and Circle B suggest

that I should take a nap. I'll dream of structured scales, pottery pieces

dug up by those who dig things.

A McDonald's for the Aeolics would

offer them a change of taste.

I'm a pink square sponge in a glazed water pail, but can no longer

recall if Greeks glazed, but they might have owned goats.

all-nighters are not good, I've heard.

it is a memory retention something most likely

studied by an isolate monk, writing in the Middle Ages

by candlelight, some monk of Greek descent.

I woke up late, I ran.

spilled black cold now coffee over my hands.

I wrote an essay, aced the test, knew the knowledge would

not stay with me long.

I closed my eyes I tried to sleep.

kouros are flipping their chitons off while

herding goats home from the hills and

trying their Levi's on.

Lycurgus didn't die, after all,

but they cut off his snaky tail.

HOME

endlessly secure comfort there

time and again over years of my life.

joy of knowing

happiness and home.

home was forever.

the place and people I could return to.

home would always be there.

in the house by the river side.

I'd watch the flow, trees, the wild life, birds.

slowly

solace would surround me,

become me.

my friend might comfort me, reassure.

if I might need it if I was bereft, broken, sad, homeless.

until.

the

day

the minute.

the seconds

home vanished.

home left me.

I was homeless

once more, and

cold like long ago.

no more solace and

no more secure

and no more.

no more.

my heart hurt.

would hurt through all time.

at the unexpected.

sudden searing

certainty of

no more

home.

in the black night of the day I knew it,

I was quiet in the early morning so as not to be heard.

I packed up

stuff.

I could not pack up

home.

hardest part.

not breathing

I shook in silent loss.

no comfort in this bereft.

covered my ferret's cage

with a white blanket, so

she would not be cold.

not me.

not me.

my rotator cuff re-broken, I

closed the patio door,

listening to the familiar sound of it sliding.

sure of.

heart bled drops in the snow I

covered up with footprints .

that was the end.

of home.

left there,

drove off down a lost expressway,

an Etheridge song plodding through my brain.

words marching in well-formed lines.

looked out the window now and then, but.

everything empty while

tears stung my eyes.

A STRANGER'S CAR

oh mom i

inhaled gravity

sucking it in to ground me.

I don't think anyone noticed

it didn't make the evening news.

standing right outside your room I held my cigarette

and smoked it down and deep and shook.

you were not much more than a long thin slice

of just this side of death,

your toenails painted chipped red, you

lost in the yellow nightie, the one that matched the bones

and hollows left of your once so beautiful face.

I willed myself back into you, so hard to nonchalantly walk in

knowing of the soon to be certainty of death. loss

shearing my heart. try to rearrange your propping pillows, and try to form

my mouth into the shapes of words that God will never count as having

mattered.

you said deb when I die will you feel bad?

and all I could do with that question was to reach out, close the windows

on the single fucking idiot birds, out there in the evening air, they

had no right. I said I did not want you to get a bronchial cough and the words I held in my mouth were sealed behind shock and silence.

I love you I love you I love you I said as I drove home in my death yellow Nova.

you have been, always been my heart, why don't you know that?

and later.

as I stood at the hospital bed petting your dead hair,

with Dick babbling on and on about "getting mommy's stuff together".

I kept wishing him to stop it, stop it. I would have kicked him in the head

just to shut him up, but I could not be further distracted. took all

my energy standing there, every cell and synapse willing you to breathe.

oh. the sobbing, the crying they did, the passing out of Kleenex and valium,

Tim and I walked out to the all black night in the all black parking lot,

we leaned against a stranger's car.

we folded our arms across our chests exactly alike, we looked into each other's eyes exactly alike,

and strained to bear the loss and pain exactly alike.

go on mom.

leave us.

damn it damn you died.

if you had stopped God's hand and looked back once,

you would have seen that

Tim and I were the only ones not crying.

JUNE FUNERAL

surreal.

drip drop Dali melting over the sides of the peach colored coffin.

turquoise sky, a black tree with no leaves, blue carnations,

pink cemetery grass. sun so hot and yellow

I felt myself melting and burning with loss.

I had needed her all of my life.

I held onto her all of my life.

I carried her worried face inside me all of my life.

she sat at the kitchen table, drinking coffee, smoking cigarettes all of my life.

now.

I can hear my heart breaking while standing in the pink grass.

it makes cracking up noises.

I walk away with Tim, holding on hard to his arm.

home.

I stare at the obituary for days, I

expect her to call me on the phone.

I will treasure her voice.

just like before,

all of my life.

TWO WOMEN

Mrs. one-breast landlady slurping hot black coffee

didn't understand a word of my

        just that day

unwed mother gives three week old baby up for adoption

        experience.

her invalid disgusting tobacco dribbling once-a-cop husband

stinks to the ceiling of this house, the carpet is a

mire around his couch bed, and he doesn't think I know

about his secretive fiddling with the 11 year old

upstairs girl, but

        I know.

the stuttering rolly second floor woman wants to know if

she can have my daughter's drinking cup, never used, and

those baby blankets, hand- me- downs. handed down to me.

        "it w-w-w-won't m-matter, will it?"

imbecile.

both of them slurp now, one at either ear of me,

they can't think of what to say and I stare into my own

black coffee, a fluid reflective hole of liquid light yawns

up at me. the blue loony-tunes bear will be so sad, he sits

        slumped in the back of my mind, and "Why?" they

want to know,

while knowing very well why, and "How could you?" while knowing very
well why I had to.

they don't

want to hear about it anyway.

All last night by the window of my attic rooms I stared,

asking the red blankety softness of the too-still and is-this-really-happening
to me

darkness for some kind of a key

too what?

I held my baby who's father's wife holds her own

two kids, this is her second marriage, and she likes me.

my baby who doesn't like bath-water is going to be beautiful one day.

break some hearts, break mine.

breaking mine.

and this early, after lunch kind of morning I threw French fries

from McDonald's to the parking lot birds because I

didn't know what else to do on my way home from the social service

everything-will-be-all-right-it-just-takes-time

agency. it will never be all right again, and I can't just yet go back upstairs
and take down

my baby's bed or I'll go mad.

two women stare at me with the sides of their heads

their eyes are stuck in the coffee.

and I have no family.

CAT

there's a tiger cat

asleep in my lap.

she does

sometimes.

when she's not eating my plants

or climbing the curtains

or chasing her tail

or frowning down at the windowsill

along the rail of the window.

ENDLESS NIGHTMARES

nothing is better than this.

sitting on the porch step with my decaf and my Basics

as the night breathes into me.

the night.

shadow fingers reach out of breezes to caress me.

I wish I could touch back,

but flesh is too heavy.

so very gently, I listen.

crickets. tree toads. cicadas.

way up in the sky,

constellations. moonlight. fireflies.

my eyes closed, my breath very deep, the smell of night to heal me.

in this joy there are no kids playing sounds, lawnmower engines,

adults shouting rages at each other.

the night is mine. lullabies sung in beautiful silence to me

in arias I could only imagine, if I imagined, in heaven.

I take my last, keep my last

longing, thankful gratefulness for all of it,

before I climb the stairs to sleep

in my bed of endless nightmares.

BOG MONSTER

Jane said I could not keep killing myself with shots and beers and bowls

of multi-colored antidepressants,

but she couldn't give me an answer when

I asked her why it mattered.

through the phone she said she was calling for help.

help?

no.

ambulance was going to take me to a flat white bed.

I ran

out the front door fast.

it was the only door I had.

ran.

running,

falling down,

getting up.

bad balance.

ran

to the woods I knew and loved, to the nature sounds of night.

trees protested, to my surprise, branches reached out to scratch my

face,

thick grasses tried to grab me, peepers stopped peeping as

I fell noisily, effortlessly, over rocks, over logs, down into the lukewarm bog

I did not see.

water and bog stink up, up to my chin as I leaked out liquor,

angering the bog monster below.

quick mud, like quick sand,

holds on.

so stuck.

grabbed and held onto by the gleeful

long unyielding liquid solid maw.

fear .

fear of dying fear

forcing me to fight back.

pull up slow.

the only thing I could think of to do.

strong, steady pulling.

what if I was wrong and pulling up was wrong and owning fear was wrong

and everything I'd never done was wrong

the dark was wrong, and running out the door was wrong,

all my choices wrong.

one foot at a time

as the bog monster sucked back fiercely, it

wanted to own me.

claim me.

took both shoes, one sock.

I have given.

for that, let me go.

battle in the dark seemed dooming, the bog water up to my nose if

I fell back I would drown no one would ever think to look in this bog to

find and bury me my bones would soak until they all dissolved or someone would some

day fill the bog with dirt and concrete for construction of some unnecessary building

I, harder, stronger, reached my arms out to grab on a final jump-up

the tall grass blades which cut my hands as I pulled myself up.

and out.

I blessed them with my blood.

sat, then.

still, cold, wet, scared.

hands bleeding, shoeless.

the summer night things had watched, waiting.

a bullfrog sounded from the over there pond,

to signal it was finished.

the bog monster had been defeated.

the oncoming train lights renewed my sense of direction, I

crawled oh so carefully to the tracks I knew well,

the gravel-steel-wood path

cutting my bare feet with carelessly strewn

by someone broken bottle glass.

I sneaked home in my bog caked clothes.

I stank like long dead frogs, dirt inside my cuts.

I threw away my war clothes

after they sat up stiff and sopped in the bathroom corner.

hand carried them to the dumpster, pressed them into garbage.

warm water soaked ,

soaped and soaped in the tub,

soap was heavenly and gently scented.

then.

slept the deepest hard sleep,

holding onto my bed

covers all the next day.

holding on to them hard,

with fists so

I could stop sinking.

JONATHAN'S DOG

maybe I'm hallucinating

now sitting all red around the rubble,

the fire in me dying, leaving me limp.

I don't know where to find you,

where to look.

we sat slow

that early spring morning with the dark porch light.

me in the hammock,

and you. swaying with some soft soon promise in your eyes.

I loved the possibility of you.

Jonathan's dog, red Labrador

was hit last night by a back –firing GM bomb spitting gas teeth

off these curbs. I swear I see his ghost limping up and down this street,

his emptiness and longing mixing with everything else underneath this
melon rind moon.

in these few seconds I would have held you tighter, my arms

enveloping you.

but I don't know where to find you,

where to look.

there is one cell's stray amino chip floating faulty.

mixes with my other acids,

breathing urgency

breathing need,

breathing the

death air of Jonathan's dog and the crashed car's

gasoline polluting left over.

I have turned over every page I own

of that one day, searching.

and still

I don't know where to find you,

where to look.

AFTER THE RIVER

I carried the yellow-green cancer inside me as I

drove the back roads home and I crammed everything

I might have felt about it down damn good.

the doctor's droning on about carcinoma, lymph nodes, chemo got

stuck behind my left ear, making the low gnat noise

the gnat clouds made in the summer at Lorraine's.

there was just then

you

and me. in New Orleans in October, early morning.

you

sat like a tourist on your proper wooden river walk bench

with our French Market loot bagged beside you. voodoo

dolls, hot garlic, a spell in a bag for dad.

you

said you wouldn't, you couldn't, the Mississippi's so

polluted, and I laughed at you and ran down past the grass

and multi-colored glass and blood stained stones that pocked

the bank all the way to the water and I

waded in. wiggled for balance on the slick green rocks, my

socks and shoes off. always before, and once again. I made this my river.

my river spot.

my own.

I pulled the smell and the feel of it

into me through my lungs to my soul and felt all rinsed away and new.

now.

driving home, I made a right turn at the stop sign and wondered,

sifting and wading through this idea of some killing thing inside me, eating.

if you'd sit up there away from me

now that I'd become polluted, too.

THE INDIANS NEXT DOOR

not always, but a pallor hangs now

inside these four walls typically. I

hide in the basement tiled in black

waiting to be scalped.

a thumping on the upstairs floor is the war cry.

here will come the screams. I

do not live here.

in the house next door I'd

sit up at the breakfast table, eggs or oatmeal,

removed. watching cartoons, where basements are for

wet clothes hung on a slack line, and not for me.

not for cowering corners webbed by artistic spiders. the

chief and his squaw would be the Indians next door,

and they would be avoided. we would not

acknowledge any right of theirs to squat on that land because

they are torturers of children and dogs.

true heathens.

and I would have no need for poetry and I would not
fear the scalping always prefaced by a dance of death.
faces need no store-bought nor home-made paint,
they already have lines.

contempt is a yellow one for my cowering in the corner.
coward.

red lines from ear to ear and
once white fangs.
I have had it. I do not live next door. I
am a heathen child, I hear the pounding drums of
loafered feet on the stairway. yes.

I have had it. red tints. hints of misplaced cheek bones
moving in. I cannot run and
I have no painted pony.

JACK'S DEATH

Bob and Donell and Don and his 23rd Wife and the kids and the dogs

listened, after Thanksgiving dinner, when all were sated with pumpkin pie,

to Eileen telling of Jack's death.

Jack, weak, shriveled, gasping, asking for a pillow.

she told.

she went to the bedroom, down the grey hall, but,

when she came back with it, he was already dead.

Not-breathing a breath dead.

there was nothing she could do for him any longer, and goddamnit,

she wouldn't be late for

her bowling league, so she left him there, dead in the dead house.

went striking and sparing and chatting and playing, sipping coke

from a cup with a straw, size 7 bowling shoe, red and white striped,

her own name etched into the round of her very specially ordered

bowling rolling down the alley ball.

Bob, Donell, sitting, staring, silent.

Drop-dead disbelief.

Bowling? She went bowling?

so happy, being happy, not saying a word about jack, no.

she told so matter-of-factly, no tears, no

sadness, see how practical she was in these matters?

No need to pay for an ambulance, no ambulance for the dead, she insisted

the coroner come, take his dead ass to the morgue.

she denied him a funeral, unnecessary she said, and besides,

nobody would come.

I think she smothered with the asked -for pillow.

NANCY

Danny stepped on the toad first, then Jeannie stepped on it again,

it's guts blew out in two long yellow squirt streams, staining the sidewalk.

Nancy was furious, made the both of them pick a spot in the back of the

back yard to dig a hole to bury the toad they had killed. toad feet would
never hop again.

I missed most of their childhood because I had to cut my hair, and because

Fred said you can't write that way all through the book. so I stopped.

Danny has OCD, and Jeannie has no memory of the toad they killed.

It is the behavior. It is the behavior that drives me crazy, Nancy exasperated

about Danny's mental illness. he's working with a counselor, he refuses
medication.

it was a chance meeting at Ray's, Nancy cut and restyled her hair, we had
not

seen each other in years. Nancy's new life, new house, new husband, new
babies

did not allow her time to include me in her life any longer. besides, I was
tattooed, I

had multiple ear piercings, would be an unwelcome influence or just
unwelcome at all

at her 5 bedroom bigger house on we-are-normal-avenue.

she was eating healthier food, she said, stopped smoking and drinking so

she would be there for her little son and twin daughters when they grew up.

we'll have to get together sometime, she said.

we never did. did not expect to. everyone says that.

six years later the overloaded truck ran the red light at Mantua and Main as Nancy

started driving through the intersection, not having a clue until last second.

the newspaper said Nancy drifted in and out of consciousness before she died,

but Tom, who knew people, said no. she was nearly decapitated instantly, her

young and injured children screaming for their mother to come alive. Jeannie

carried the other children out of the car and safe away so the

jaws of life could come try to, what? save the dead? cops and the

firemen sheeted around the car. Danny was not there. I imagined

him getting the phone call or the knock on the door, and cringed for him.

I did not go to the funeral.

reasoned myself sensibly out of it, it would be an intrusion

if she no longer wanted me in her life,

she would not want me in her death. messing it up.

I watched it from afar, hiding myself in the old part of the cemetery

by the river, behind the tombstones of those I did not know.

when the many mourners and family had all gone, I walked to the grave and sat

among the still fragrant flowers. I stopped my heart, emptied my mind, extending out to find

her energy. there was no welcome there. energy without acceptance only.

Tom said when he drove by, he saw rays from heaven

shining brightly on her tomb dirt.

Tom sees stuff like that.

but even so, if it was true

I did not care.

JACK'S WIFE

it was a goddamn good death.

cancer of the liver.

Don gave me the news at the mall where I was Christmas shopping

and he was moving some store's boxes up on top of each one

below it.

"just before Thanksgiving."

he looked hard at me to see my non-reaction.

well, what, Don? did you expect me to give a shit?

still.

to know for sure was comforting, far more than I expected

it to be.

everything Jack .

did in his life caused some other person pain.

he never carried a kindness or empathy toward any living thing.

I thought about Jack's wife, free of him at last and alone in the house

with his clothes and his stink and his ghost and his name, sorting

out for the salvation army.

me and she and he had not one fond thing to remember.

she was scrubbing down his kitchen chair, mixing bleach with some soapy

cleanser.

but.

there was

in me.

one remaining.

angry thinking.

I never had or took the chance to stand up in his face to tell him

he was an unredeemable, child raping, dog beating bastard.

and.

I hated him.

I would, could, might have

called him

rage provoking names

in a long breathless on and on string.

miserable, lily-livered, heartless, non-essential, implausible, ignorant, callous, bile colored, paralytic

unnecessary, swine related, sociopathic, un-empathetic, panty hoarding, perverted, slime sucking,

monster who never should have occupied space on this earth.

he would have tried to beat me with his fists if I had ever the

guts.

to say it.

but.

I never had the

guts

to say it.

I had always always just.

been so all soaked through with

afraid.

so much never wanting to see him again in my life

afraid.

POLICE PISTOL

It was the best gun.

better than all the colts, 22's, 9 mm's in the gun case.

"police pistol" the man said. "very good choice."

the pearled handle in my thin palm

the beautifully holster polished black barrel.

I was in love with my gun

I played with it, especially when

I drank my Cutty Sark and Jameson's.

I dry fired at my head, looking into the wall mirror.

an awful weight is born when no one comes to cradle you.

on the shooting range I rolled in ecstasy, felt the recoil, real bullets.

I shot the cardboard head.

I shot the cardboard heart.

I shot the cardboard eyeball out.

Beatles said happiness was a warm gun.

I don't know why it came up to me out of the emptiness,

but I sadly knew I was living in breathlessness.

everything just hurt all the time too much, a pressing weight.

finally unbearable.

I loaded the gun with 2 bullets and spun the barrel.

as I pressed the gun against my head, I thought about my cousins.

Tim hung himself on New Year's Eve from a tree in Connecticut.

Bobby blew his brains all over his girlfriend's wall, even after he swore

to god and promised his father he would never do that.

my uncle was so bereft he went on to drink himself to death.

fat Susie, who did not deserve it, inherited everything.

I pulled the trigger once, aiming at the place I imagined my brains would be

so I would never have to remember anything ever again.

did I have brains, or only a brain?

one brain.

not plural.

I spun the barrel again.

Christopher Walken played Russian Roulette all the time in the movie

called "The Deer Hunter", and he lived for a long time, people crowding,

placing bets.

I pulled the trigger again so I would never have to remember anything one
more time.

but my brain did not blow out and scatter the wall paint.

I had my eyes wide open, watching so I know it did not happen.

I had a beautiful gun full of betrayal.

with explosive anger in my hands I threw my gun down hard on the floor.

it came alive for me then, shooting a hole in my left stereo speaker.

I was left bereft like my uncle, so much so that

I could hear the stars moan.

SECOND TIME

first time

I came to you my hands holding an empty pepsi bottle.

I sat it down on your kitchen counter, I

couldn't

help it.

your black eyes flash as you study me, I

really didn't know about Hudson, you.

if you had seen my face the day you called me,

you would honestly be sure and secure of my truth.

now, you only know the truth of me.

your littlest baby lies so skinny on the couch, so still,

she knows she cannot interrupt.

third time, party.

wasn't it?

I cannot be sure.

so quickly we all smoked, stoned, space changes, my

mind in sections, quartered like a peeled and pulled apart grapefruit.

the stairway carpet led me, carried me up

the stairs, to the bed where I sat and shook, I

can't explain it now. I was terrified, the night was tall,

you mocked me with your blackness, intentionally hurting me with it.

you laughed,

"hey,girl" is what you called me.

a gentle curse that filled the room with your lips.

a hissed between your perfect teeth, your head far

back in the white cased pillow.

pride. resentment.

I cannot bear your passion,

it burns me inside.

you tell me of your sister,

who doesn't like me.

you hold my hand, you slap my face,

you can't make up your mind.

and Hudson grows more weary with the days as

he turns up the collar of his coat and drinks cheap wine like a medicine.

he does not have secrets any longer.

THE MUFFIN

in grade school, second grade.

I fisted through the noon lunch trash in my homeless orphan

filthy tattered dress that was ugly.

I was looking for Walt's lunch muffin.

he didn't eat it. I saw him toss it there with

kid-mouth smeared paper napkins.

at least a dozen kids or so watched me find it, pull it out,

begin to eat it.

they said you pig you hog trash food will kill you

make you die. and I so hungry and humiliated, waited.

SHADOWS

I must be quiet in this place of shadows

or no one will come .

I will live in the darknesses I know.

they are printable.

I reach out for a thousand words,

or maybe just enough to fill my outstretched hands.

not talking is shrinking and not disturbing the coon hound.

my hands are tired and empty,

I have begged for expression that never comes

and I feel all wet about it, dark water

drops from my brow and

the dark strands of my wet hair

quietly, drop by drop.

once I tried to take a picture

with my camera

of giant spider webs backlit by the bright porch light.

it came out shadows on black film, I have

wondered if I might be

shadows on black film.

PRAYER

arms stretched up and out with empty hands.

never mind it.

I will.

will my love for them out into the universe, close to

creation. If I was ever sure of myself in my being, in

my uncertain certainties of chemistry, physics. energies of

rotting and crying and sobbing and dying. souls.

of my family dead recently and long times ago would

one sunny or snowy day or night absorb me after a day or a

decade or more.

we would mingle, mix, stop being.

so separated.

some time, over there across the side street by

the old slave tunnels dug out of the ledges. I

will tell, and they will know that I have wrung out the sun, and

it cannot be more sacred than that so.

amen and

amen and

amen.

SALEM

through sunglasses I censored the market,

Black staring fish on ice for sale .

piles of blacker bananas on carts and tables—

Everybody comes to see and spend,

Chinese mother's baby cries out at the smell of fresh fish, and the stink

of the drunken, snoring bum I almost stepped on.

Homeless.

his beard needs mowed. Glass bottles of empty around him,

sidewalk litter.

a woman down a side street in a pink dress, sashaying to the music I don't hear,

I have the rolling around train wheels in my head.

Later,

sitting solo on the park bench where someone wrote a phone number

in red ink, and underneath it said "good sex"

white swan boats stand on the water in a bobbing line, I

wish that I could sail away when a pimp from the Combat Zone

disturbs my reverie. asks do I want good dope?

I finger the rock in my pocket I picked out of Walden Pond,

my hand made a hole in the water there.

Fred said "when you go there, stay out of the Combat Zone."

Donnie said "when you get into town, stay away from the Combat Zone."

I heard Fred, I heard Donnie, but I

didn't listen, did not behave.

boys crammed into a phone booth for dollars, boys

in and out all day long. X-rated movies shout from make- me -blind

movie marquees, come see me, come here, see me.

high spike heeled women sidle up, I don't like their touch, want me.

dope in a bag with buds,

pills in a baggie, they look just like candy. Uppers, downers, for out of towners,

like me, just like me.

Salem , Danvers, Salem, wherever the

witches were hung.

high on the hill, it's a playground now, such a sacrilege.

when the snow came in May, I decided to stay inside and sleep.

I didn't have a coat I could wear. they weren't really witches

anyway, I was drinking too much beer. Had rye in it, I think.

hysterical girls had fun with farmer's wives, it

was a long ago puritan fest, I saw it all behind my eyes as the

schools closed and the plows came and the lights went out.

no electricity.

FRENCH QUARTER BOOKSTORE

I had seen a room like this before.

Susan's or Brady's, in the folds of my hometown.

a near replica, bookshelves lining both badly wall-papered side walls,

books crammed inside them, side up and on top flat, pages sticking out here, untidy.

Tom left already, wondered why. but he never was a reader.

a couch, a chair, an end table on top an ugly lime carpet remnant in

the middle of the room but, no one was sitting or reading. the only other person in the store was behind the front glass counter, man I had not seen.

silent.

staring.

spoke.

asked me if I might like a cup of tea. free tea?

was that odd? I thought it might be, I told him I was not going to stay, needed to see where Tom went, he

said I could take it with me, the tea, the free tea, in a white to-go Styrofoam cup, as he took the tea ball out. I tasted first, a quick sip to see if I liked it

had a nutty curl to it, colored hot gold.

thanked him, left.

momentary worry.

Tom.

there he was, way down there at the end of the block, leaning on a stop sign like he was posing for a camera shot.

sipped my tea slowly, I would have preferred ice tea in this August

New Orleans heat. closer, I saw his face troubled and nearly angry.

Tom?

he said throw the tea down. but I like it.

throw the tea down now, or I will knock it out of your hand.

I threw the tea down now.

why?

didn't you feel the energy in that place?

energy? no.

I felt guilty for not feeling it. he grabbed me by the arm, rushing us across the street. he had never grabbed my arm before.

Tom?

whatever they are doing there is evil. said he felt it right away, could barely breathe,

had to rush out into the stifling heat, could not take the time to bring me with him.

oh. I'm sorry. for what, I did not know.

back to our hotel room, the cool air conditioning was not only refreshing, but necessary. I pushed my hot hair away from my sweating brow, reminded Tom we needed to be up by six. dinner, then the vampire tour for intelligent people. I kicked

off my shoes, thinking about the vampires we had seen sprawled out on the

grassy places by the Mississippi river bank. mostly teen-agers, dressed in black, wearing shades, pointy caps on their teeth. how did they get jobs? slept quickly, saw the man from the bookstore in my dreams, he was shape-shifting.

Why?

slept too long, vampire tour first, then eat late. it was a good plan as my stomach felt grey. I chewed up 3 raspberry tums.

walking the Quarter with my brother, past the smallest A+P, aisles very narrow.

Fred said he had never liked the word "very" very much. I wondered what funny things he'd have to say about the vampires. would he say "funny" or "very funny"? or something else?

I noticed I had put my hand on Tom's shoulder before. now, crooked walking. I'm okay, just a balance problem. a block later I knew

I was not okay.

Tom.

not okay.

can't walk good.

something really wrong.

all the strength that used to be mine

was leaking out a hole and onto the sidewalk, which eagerly accepted it.

Tom.

help.

help me walk back.

we turned around, toward the hotel. back there, back there.

tourists, teens, toddlers, townies, staring at me.

please don't do that.

I leaned on Tom pitifully, but my legs were all the way gone, I had wiggly lime jello legs. we'd walk some, he'd sit me down.

walk some.

sit me down.

and down.

and down.

lime green jello legs.

I fell into the hotel room.

dying.

I crawled as a baby might, on my wiggly knees and watery hands,

held on hard to the sink edge to pull myself up, rinse the sweat pouring off

my face, dripping like a sudden rain. slid all the way back down the cool wall
to the floor.

so this was

dying.

melting

and fading away.

Tom

pulled me to the bed, wet sheet I had become.

eyes sinking into my face, soon they would be all gone too.

Tom's earlier anger shadowed his usually pleasant features.

Tom.

don't leave me here when I am dead. take me back on the train.

tracks. clickety-clack. on the track.

take me home, 'kay?

it was so simple

just to unbecome.

lose legs.

brain slides out one ear.

pulse slows.

Tom reached down and shook me.

Why?

no matter what, he said, with slow, strong, deliberate force, you focus on

one thing.

what Tom?

over and over and over you say to yourself, "I walk in the light of the Lord."

"Lord?"

he closed my eyes, told me focus, repeat.

I walk, no I don't, I fall down.

I all fall down. light.

light.

in the light. of the walk.

I walk in.

focus.

dying.

here.

walk in the Lord.

in the light I.

walk in the light. Lord.

I walk in the light of the Lord.

over and over and over.

I heard Tom's voice far away in another land, speaking words

I could not understand because of the light of the Lord I was walking in.

space behind my eyes brightened.

it was the light.

the light of the Lord.

it was peaceful, and I was comforted.

years, peaceful ones, passed

before I opened my eyes.

Tom?

did I die?

no.

did you save me?

I prayed for the return of your soul.

where did it go?

silence.

Tom?

can I sleep without dying?

Yes.

so I slept.

without dying and

the man from the bookstore

did not return to my to my dreams.

THE DINING CHAIRS

she sits, skin stuck to the green backed vinyl dining chairs,

collecting and counting his money as the blue boatman talks to

her from her always on soap opera t.v.

one half a spoon-scooped cantaloupe lays dead on a saucer,

it's orange eye chewed up between her brown and yellow teeth.

cup of coffee, cold, one drifting air hair captured

on the red lipstick smeared cup rim.

she had always worn bright, too bright, red lipstick,

but her under-arm hair was a foot long. I often thought about braiding it.

she has sat in that same spot, different dining chairs over all the years

since her wedding day. washing clothes once a week on Sunday,

bleaching out shit streaked underwear, dropping clothespins all

over the ground as she stretches out the sheets, pinching the socks.

she's always running to or from something.

running to the grocery

running to the bank to count the money

running up the credit cards

til

he beat her for his impotence.

he beats her just for fun.

she wears tent dresses I could camp in,

cooking cabbage, cooking meatloaf to serve to

him on breakable, bold-patterned plates.

he never looks at her.

he doesn't care.

I wonder if she hated him as she watched him eat,

watched him hold the knife and fork, cut and spit and chew.

wishing him dead twenty years ago.

now.

as she counts his money, she is lucky

not to be contaminated with him any longer.

PIECES

I was sitting in my chair where love once laid waiting,

I did not know about it being there.

you were wrapped up in whispers, oceans away, you did not call me

and I could not guess how you were living.

often, a silver chill ran through the room,

I was not aware it was an omen.

one day.

you came back across the oceans, I

saw you standing in the kitchen by the sink. I

only wanted to welcome you,

hug you home,

but you were not receptive.

you held me the length of your right arm away from you.

it was unbearable.

I could not remember, what had I done?

it was the beginning of breaking down without your knowledge.

Jerry said Kathleen could not do it by herself, and

as he always added, "what's the matter with you?"

and Gayle said, "Kathleen and I cannot do it by ourselves." and,

added a touch of her own making.

"you better get over it."

it. it was an it.

so I wondered about what was the matter with me,

and why had it always been the same matter, instead of, maybe

a different one, like anger management, but that could not be ruled out, as

I had started to scream at all my employees lately.

no more patient explaining,

as had been my way.

to instruct and give reasons

was

gone.

I screamed with rage at a fat maid I found sitting, filing

her nails.

room reservation came storming and slamming and fuming and cussing

and parking,

advised him to take a flying leap, as my trainee observed.

each morning I woke up, saw you mostly in the kitchen maybe once in the,

yes.

in the living room, you turned your head away from me and back,

said no.

no.

I don't have time.

you stared me in the face, waiting for me to dare say another word about it.

I did not say anything, I just

stopped.

scared to dare.

closed the curtains to make it dark,

didn't want light.

didn't have light.

didn't own light.

scared of light.

the day of your wedding,

I fled.

scared of your wedding.

scared of you.

with Tom to the waterfall hidden but heard in the deep park woods.

we tried to remember if he had ever had this matter wrong with him,

but he could not remember if it was the exact matter.

maybe something close to being this or that. he

may not have understood anything I said while throwing pebbles in the
water, but

he was the only one who listened while skipping stones.

I could, well.

I could live with Tom. but

it might have fried grandma, she was addicted to valium, then

there was dad. always getting in the way.

we

would have all made a nice photograph, standing up together,

but Tom and dad

were always mad at each other.

when dad came home for summer vacation from the race track

he took me over to Neil's to break a horse

Bobby tried to ride once and got thrown off of.

when I broke the horse, I had bruised back bones and a slammed head, still, we celebrated around the kitchen table with many bottles of home brew.

Bobby was not there, he tended the plants hidden between the flowering tomatoes.

I could not share anything with you, though.

I desperately slept in the deliberately darkened room.

put earplugs in.

no noise.

no input.

no output.

rotting from the inside out seemed like a good thing to do,

it hurt a lot,

but it did not make noise.

one

half

of

one

hour

with you.

us

talking to each other.

you explaining your lack of time.

you holding me home and

glad to see me, too

would not have been that much.

for you to do.

it would have meant everything to me.

I might have opened the curtains to light again, and

welcomed noise.

maybe,

 put my fell off already pieces

back on.

but you did not.

and I did not.

and we never did.

THE ANGELS AND GAYLE

the angels were not there for her when Gayle died.

it was a death so sudden, how do they calculate death miles

in order to be on time?

what messenger gives them word?

but, surely, it happened often.

always happened.

guillotines caused sudden death, the indifferent beheadings by

Henry the VIII, car wrecks on the highways, heart attacks

while alone in the house, and so on and on

throughout all the years of our so often cruel history.

maybe they flew into the great beyond we are so sure and unsure of,

and captured sudden death souls, spirits waiting, momentarily lost.

I sat on the other bed when they finally arrived too late. I shook inside and,

more visibly outside, even in their heavenly presence. I watched.

as did the angels, when Billie faked grief at Gayle's sudden death.

I had wanted to slap her for years, but I could not make myself stand

up.

the angels disappeared.

three of them.

there.

not there.

maybe a great many angels had been recently laid off, not

allowed to do angel duties for a while. why

would that happen?

not there to lift up softly the energy we all give up eventually.

thoughts of angels hurried off when fake Billie fakely stroked

Gayle's really dead forehead.

At least Gayle's father had the good sense

not to come into the death room at all, he.

knew.

he would break and cry.

"she did not die alone."

Sheila told me as she scooted up by my side as if to share a secret

which was not one. she'd told everyone how she was there at Gayle's side,

holding her hand when she died, but Sheila lied.

Liar.

that's what lying liars do. they lie.

she needed slapping, too, for her self- heralded heroics.

Gayle died while the nurse's aide bathed her, and for that last

act, Sheila was not allowed to be in the room.

If the angels came back for any reason, I did not see them, which

only means

I did not see them.

I closed my eyes,

no one noticed no one ever does.

I prayed a shaking prayer for

the angels to find Gayle, and lift her up to a place she could just rest.

at last.

not to worry about paying bills while working for minimum wage.

FATEFUL DAY

the night before, tucked safe in bed,

I tucked my new toy under the doily on the nightstand

so it wouldn't get cold.

Eileen kissed me goodnight, walked out the door, turned off the light.

next morning.

Eileen ran into my room threw open the blinds with fury

grabbed my head hair to use as a handle as

she bounced me up and down on the floor, I

had turned into a round orange basketball in the night.

she bounced me with glee, dancing around me like

a savage till my spine tried to climb out the top of my head.

when fury spent.

she left me there.

on the wood floor screaming.

shock.

shock.

shock.

why?

my four-year-old world shattered around me.

not.

not.

not.

understanding.

and so it began.

CLAIRE'S SISTER

she is the first to know the secret I did not know.

she beat me with it

as we walked along the great surprise of riverbank.

tall grasses growing.

Claire's fat sister staring.

me and Billy laughed, both of us drunk, all the way

to the nunnery and back about her fat fatness.

I decided to suck my breath inside and never let it go.

trying to race the dirt bikes faster, hoping, maybe

even to crash on the cinder road. I just wanted

out.

she took us to the five and dime store all the time,

plying us with one cent candy.

Billy was my best friend in all the time that did not mean much.

one fierce day,

I grabbed her by the neck and choked her.

not to death.

fat folds around her neck crinkled.

she did not fight back with her fat hands,

but stared at me fiercely at the farmer's breakfast table

for the next two days

while eating eggs and bacon and biscuits with gravy.

the gravy running out and down the corners of her mouth.

like slop.

THE LAST TIME I SAW EILEEN

look at her.

the mighty Eileen down.

flat on her back in the ICU white hospital bed.

mouth an open hollow, tongue coated with thrush,

pinned to her tubes trailing out of every orifice,

hooked up to blipping, bleeping monitors and screens.

I came to torture. I came to taunt.

I came to gloat, and laugh with glee.

I came to dance.

I came to celebrate.

I came to see her helplessness.

I brought no card, no fat bouquet of flowers.

there was no love in my heart, in fact,

I did not care.

don said it was a stroke, at first. Eileen, upset.

seeking comfort away from Helen, who roared at her like a thunder.

Eileen sought solace in her garden, watering thirsty plants until she

fell face first into the prized one she loved so much,

called it

the bleeding heart.

after the stroke ambushed her, after the ambulance rode her away to the

hospital bed, her heart attacked her, gleefully gushing out blood from

long-clogged veins she probably got from eating moldy food and empty

and evaporated eggs

we found later, in her fridge.

I stood alone with her.

stood over her bed, got down in her face and yelled

"MOM!"

because I could.

because I wanted her to wake up and be aware of my intended torment.

all the monitors moaned, sending pulse and breathing levels off

all the charts and screens and ran them up the wall.

wall art.

nurses rushing in, told me, no, you can't upset her.

can't? can't?

I could.

I could take hold of her bedside water pitcher, pour the cold

all the way down her throat till she spit and choked and gurgled,

snot hanging out her nose on the end of one of her long nose hairs.

throat thrush liquefied, wondered if she'd drown, while I'd stand by silent, watching,

wondering if I'd waste my one great chance, when

no.

not that song.

wrong song.

Elton John began to sing "The One" over the hospital piped in radio station.

the unwanted unnecessary song

with its' unneeded words

stopped me when it shouldn't have

stopped me at all.

it did not apply.

I sat.

down.

in the brunette chair,

listening to the familiar words.

"I never thought you'd come."

I needed a double shot of Daniels.

"I never thought you'd come."

I sat still, a stone sat still.

stones often do.

till the full moon filled the sky, sending some of its' moon beams

in, through the darkened window, washing over me and the nearly dead Eileen.

nurses said time to go.

time to go, Pink Floyd.

"time to go".

visitation is over, over, over.

visit?

this was not a visit.

I was not visiting.

I came to see the sick and evil bitch.

I came to spit on her wizened face.

I came to stone to death, using unkind

words as my weapon.

I had done nothing.

nothing.

I rose from my chair,

an anguish fell out on the floor.

I picked it up, was that dust that on it?

I put it in my pocket.

I kissed eileen's forehead,

said a whispered prayer for her peace.

the heart monitor relaxed.

I left her.

alone. I

knew there would be no need to

ever go back there.

We hope you enjoyed this book.

Please visit our web site for other great books.

WWW.BadgleyPublishingCompany.com

Made in the USA
Columbia, SC
01 June 2024

36456879R00148